Unravelling the Yarn

*Zoë Hart Dyke née Bond
and
the Leyton Silk Road*

Claire Weiss

© Claire Weiss, Leyton, London E10. 2018

Published by Leyton & Leytonstone Historical Society 2018

www.leytonhistorysociety.org.uk
www.leytonpast.info
www.facebook.com/LeytonHistorySociety

Printed at Aldgate Press, London

Although every effort has been made to contact all copyright holders, the sources of some images are obscure. The publication of any material on which due clearance is not seen to have been sought or given is unintentional. I will be glad to make corrections needed in any future editions.

I am indebted to Derek Cook, David Boote and the Hart Dyke family for their interest and support but at the same time, the views expressed, the approach and ideas in this book remain entirely my own responsibility, as do any errors or omissions.

ISBN 978-1-9998278-3-0

Contents

Foreword		5
Introduction		7
Chapter One:	The Bonds come to Leyton	11
Chapter Two:	The Bonds move on	20
Chapter Three:	Mulberry trees and silkworms	26
Chapter Four:	Zoë's youth	30
Chapter Five:	Marriage	35
Chapter Six:	The Hart Dyke line continues	39
Chapter Seven:	Zoë and Oliver's partnership	42
Chapter Eight:	Inheritance of Lullingstone	45
Chapter Nine:	The peaks of achievement	49
Chapter Ten:	Zoë's challenges	54
Chapter Eleven:	Lullingstone in the 1940s	61
Chapter Twelve:	Hertfordshire and beyond	66
Chapter Thirteen:	Zoë's sponsors and influences	71
Chapter Fourteen:	Dr & Mrs Bond and Leyton-born offspring	79
Chapter Fifteen:	What to make of Zoë	87
Selected Bibliography and References		93
Appendix 1:	The Bonds: an outline ancestry	100
Appendix 2A:	The Hart Dykes: an outline ancestry	101
Appendix 2B:	Dates of Hart Dyke baronetcies	102
Appendix 2C:	Baronetcies and inheritance	103
Appendix 3A – E:	Manor Road, Leyton	104
Appendix 4:	Extracts from *Paulina*	109
Appendix 5	*Porter v Bond*, 1873	111
End Notes		113
Alphabetical Index		123
Acknowledgements		127

Fig. 1: Zoe Lady Millicent Hart Dyke (née Bond), born at 9 Manor Road, Leyton, Essex.[1]
Pictured here on the staircase of Lullingstone Castle, 1952.
© National Portrait Gallery image 126630

Foreword

Cllr Yemi Osho, Mayor of Waltham Forest 2017 - 18

From modest beginnings in Leyton, Zoë Lady Hart Dyke's fascination with silkworms, which began at the age of just four, culminated in supplying silk for Queen Elizabeth's coronation robes.

The life of Zoë Lady Hart Dyke is a remarkable if not overly well-known one. I am, therefore, delighted that Claire Weiss has written this biography of one of Waltham Forest's most notable and inspiring women.

She overcame a lack of academic achievement and developed her highly specialised technical skills and knowledge of the production of silk into nationally important milestones in the creation of a complex and demanding commercially-operational silk farm.

Zoë Lady Hart Dyke's life-long passion led her to become a respected and leading expert in sericulture and a successful author. Like many high-achieving women, Zoë Lady Hart Dyke's trajectory did not go unchallenged. However, her extraordinary track record is so relevant for us today in the way that she associated with and celebrated fellow women pioneers in the fields of media, theatre, architecture, art and craftwork.

Her life story is a glimpse into the mid-century cultural developments straddling Art-Deco with Modern and it is an amazing example of feminist success that has yet to be fully celebrated.

It is fitting, therefore, that Lady Dyke's story should be written by an industrious, local campaigner and author with an eye for detail and a determination to capture the history and heritage of the borough's past. Claire has spent three years researching and writing this book and her commitment shows through on every page.

I am particularly pleased that the Leyton and Leytonstone Historical Society is publishing *Unravelling the Yarn: Zoë Hart Dyke née Bond and the Leyton Silk Road* to coincide with the 2018 marking of International Women's Day and the centenary of the first women in the UK receiving the right to vote. She has left society with a legacy of how to achieve the impossible.

I offer my sincere congratulations to Claire on this work and I hope you, the reader, will enjoy the story of an inspirational woman.

Introduction

With no reason other than to learn more about the history of a local house in Manor Road, Leyton in which I had lived for ten years, I found that to my surprise I had become interested in the life of the late Zoë Lady Hart Dyke (née Bond). Born as Millicent Zoë Bond, she was the youngest child of Dr Barnabas Mayston Bond and Mrs Eliza Bond (née Luxon) and came into the world in 1896 at 9 Manor Road, Leyton, Essex; the precise house in which seventy-five years later my husband Len and I were to start our own family. Possibly there is a clue in the title of Zoë's autobiographical *So Spins the Silkworm*[2] that some details in her book may be a kind of 'tale spun' rather than history told. My fascination with her life-story grew as I uncovered elements that perhaps had been over-glorified or glossed over.

Zoë was to become successful in establishing and running a unique silk farm at Lullingstone Castle in Kent, later transferring to Ayot St Lawrence in Hertfordshire. From the 1930s to the 1950s, silk yarn, albeit in small quantities, was produced under her supervision for onward despatch to the high-quality spinners and fabric manufacturers of the day. The origins of this enterprise apparently lay in Zoë's own fascination, from early childhood, with silkworms and their productive characteristics.[3]

Knowing that there had been a large, ancient mulberry tree at the time of my own family's residing at 9 Manor Road (Fig. 27), my imagination took hold. Realising from its appearance that this magnificent old tree would have been standing there during the 1890s[4] and appreciating that the leaf of the mulberry was the preferred diet of the silkworm, I became intrigued as to whether Zoë's interest in these creatures had perhaps begun here in Leyton.

Zoë's autobiography includes much botanical, zoological and technical detail, and I was to learn from her, at first with some disappointment, that silkworms thrive best on the white mulberry. Being aware that the tree in Manor Road was the black variety I had been taking it for granted that silkworms were happy to feed on any type of mulberry leaves. I nevertheless consoled myself a little, when consulting the autobiography further, to find that Zoë herself admitted to feeding silkworms on all manner of vegetation, including lettuce or endive, whenever the need arose! And feeding them on black mulberry, she noted, is not unusual at the end of seasons, when it simply produces a coarser variety of silk.[5]

I still like to imagine Zoë as an infant in the long back garden of 9 Manor Road in the 1890s, playing under the mulberry tree there and gaining an interest in the life of insects. My own children Angela and Ivan were to get up to climbing adventures decades later on the mulberry tree at that first family home of ours in Manor Road. A photograph is at Fig. 28. A 'Fairy Bluebell' was said to live there!

Fig. 2: 'Children and mulberry tree.'
Sketch by Ellen Buxton, Leytonstone House 1864.[6]

An earlier local sketch at Fig. 2 captures something of the interaction between children and another local mulberry tree in Victorian times. And Fig. 3 shows that very same mulberry tree more than 140 years later.

I was soon to acquire more than botanical knowledge as I became increasingly curious about the life and achievements of the intriguing Millicent Zoë. I delved beyond the autobiography, and explored other literature, articles and public records relating to the Bond family, their in-laws, ancestors and descendants, and later engaged with existing members of her Hart Dyke family.

I discovered that, after she had enjoyed the remarkable novelty of being a single wage-earning young woman in cosmopolitan west London during and after the First World War, Zoë appeared to have been abandoned by her parents: they left the country reportedly for the south of France. Zoë was later excluded from her mother's will, but so was her father Dr Barnabas Mayston Bond.

Furthermore, it was not only from her Bond family that Zoë became estranged: I found that, at the time of the publication of her autobiography in 1949, the 53-year-old Zoë was by then no longer part of the Hart Dyke baronetcy[7] into which she had married – twice – in the early 1920s. I realised that I was also stumbling across both an undisclosed wedding ceremony and a sad divorce.

Introduction

I was beguiled by the opening words in a chapter of *An Englishman's Home*[8] by Zoë's grandson Tom Hart Dyke:

> "Grandma Zoë's great good fortune – apart from being strikingly beautiful, hugely persuasive, inexhaustibly energetic and married to my grandfather … was to have vast reserves of charm and cheek."

I followed Zoë's progress through her unconventional life in which she circulated with fashionable media and arts people, with intellectuals, with leading businesswomen, the military and royalty in the inter-war Art-Deco period and beyond.

Fig. 3: *The Buxton House mulberry tree, Leytonstone, 2005.*
Photo, courtesy of David Boote, reveals the gnarled, spread development over the 140 years since this tree was sketched (Fig. 2).

As a result, my originally-intended 'house history' of 9 Manor Road will be a separate, more modest account. The starting point of this work now is the story of the first residents of the house, Dr and Mrs Bond and family, their life in Leyton, how they got there and whence they moved. With the story spanning the end of the Victorian years and the first half of the twentieth century, I will then focus on unravelling the extraordinary life of their daughter Millicent Zoë, touching on aspects of social mobility, gender and class in the historical periods encountered.

The account concludes with an appraisal of Zoë's achievements as a pioneer of creative manufacturing industry, and at the same time adds insights to her character as revealed by the impressions she left on others including her family and associates.

Chapter One: The Bonds come to Leyton

Leyton, Essex, in the nineteenth century

According to *A History of the County of Essex: Volume 6*,[9] Leyton remained rural until the mid-nineteenth century. The opening of railways to London with stations at Lea Bridge (1840 – see Fig. 9) and Low Leyton (1856), followed by the provision of other forms of mass transport, were key triggers in Leyton's change in character from rural to urban. At the same time the rapidly expanding opportunities for employment in offices, in industry, and in infrastructure enterprises, particularly railways, both in London and in the areas around Leyton, transformed the village by the end of the nineteenth century into a suburban dormitory for clerks and manual workers. The old civil parish was formed into an Urban District within Essex in 1894, just two years before Zoë was born.

Once speculative development had begun, Leyton ceased to attract the wealthy residents of the metropolis who formerly might have migrated there in search of rural seclusion.[10] In their place came new influxes of people who were not so well-off. I found that some were from further afield, for instance from Essex and East Anglia, and others were working-class families from east London.[11] Enterprising estate developers, in areas such as rural Leyton, were parcelling up the plots of farms or large houses. Newcomers were housed in the newly-built rows of yellow-brick two-storey terraced houses and larger villas configured mostly in rectangular street formations.

Manor Road, Leyton

Manor Road was part of this intensive late nineteenth-century urban development. Its southern half, below the crossroads with the much older Capworth Street, was designed with a broad carriageway. With other neighbouring streets, such as Vicarage Road and Grange Park Road featuring some individually-designed plots, Manor Road was distinctive for the length of its uniform terraces. The generous width of the sites, some twenty feet, and the good-sized gardens at the front and the back, some of ninety feet, were the environment in which the first occupants of No. 9 Manor Road took up residence. See diagram at Fig. 6.

Early occupants: the Bond Family

Dr Barnabas Mayston Bond (born in 1862), whose family originated in Alburgh, southern Norfolk, and his wife Eliza Josephine Bond (née Luxon, born in 1860) with origins in St Merryn, Cornwall, were almost certainly the first permanent residents of 9 Manor Road. The earliest evidence of their residence is an 1888 entry in the Medical Register for Dr Bond which was an update to his 1887 entry. That 1887 entry had recorded his name at an address of 4 Freelands Road, Bromley, Kent.[12]

This Kent address was that of his mother, the widow Rebecca Ann Bond,[13] at the time of her death. She had died on 28 October 1887 leaving the considerable sum of £3,926.8s.7d.[14][15] Barnabas appears to have left Kent for Leyton fairly soon after his mother's demise. For the family tree diagram see Appendix 1: The Bonds: an outline ancestry - diagrammatic view.

The decision in 1888 of Barnabas Mayston Bond to move into Leyton only a year after medically qualifying might be seen as that of an "urban seeker of rural seclusion" as described by historians of the locality[16] since, although his roots were in the country, Barnabas Mayston from a fairly young age had lived in central London. Admittedly, Leyton was no longer an isolated rural village environment, but its location in Essex on the border of the Lea Valley continued to give it the aura of being in the countryside. It is also possible that Barnabas Mayston plumped for Leyton in order to further a particular career route requiring further medical study, something that will be considered in Chapter Two. Certainly its location on a railway line to Cambridge and with links to Norfolk would have facilitated journeys north-eastwards.

Connections in London

Looking back to 1881, the census had recorded at 21 Doughty Street, St Pancras, London (now in Camden)[17] a household comprising widow Rebecca Ann Bond as head, the 19-year-old Barnabas Mayston as son and medical student, and his sister Mary Patten Bond. Rebecca Ann's living was noted as "income from property", a status that evidently sustained the immediate family and supported the employment of a resident cook and housemaid.[18] Rebecca Ann's late husband was Barnabas Bond the elder, fifteen years her senior. She had been his second wife. He was aged 60 when our leading character Barnabas Mayston was born, and he had died on 28 December 1872 at Alburgh, leaving a sum of up to £6,000.[19][20]

A contested legacy

Thus Barnabas Mayston had been only ten years old at the time of his father's death and, along with his only sibling, Mary Patten, eventually would be in a position to benefit from the sizeable legacy due to his mother. However, that legacy had not gone unchallenged. One year after having been widowed in 1872, Rebecca Ann, together with son Barnabas Mayston and with one George Henry Porter, were defendants in a 'Cause' at Chancery[21] whereby the Bond legacy was contested by a Mary Porter – the childless wife of said George Henry Porter. (See Fig. 4 which illustrates one of the thirteen pages of the Cause.) Note that Rebecca Ann, as can be seen in the family tree diagram at Appendix 1, does not seem to have been a traditional farmer's wife: she was the daughter of a Kentish Town solicitor, James Patten. This fact may help to explain how she was in a position to defend this legal challenge by Mary Porter.

The background was that Barnabas Bond the elder had been made an executor of the will of a Rev. John Mills. This bachelor clergyman had been born in 1808 and was listed

Chapter One

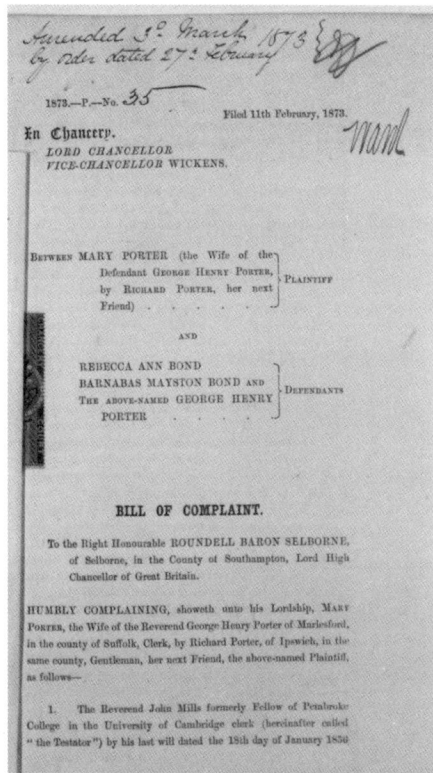

Fig. 4: Title page of Porter v Bond, 1873. The National Archives (TNA) C16/884/P35.

in the 1851 census and elsewhere as a Fellow of Pembroke College, Cambridge. Given both the complexity and the size of the legacy, which clearly had facilitated Rebecca Ann to move from Norfolk back to her London origins, I wondered how it was that Barnabas Bond the elder had become executor to this Rev. Mills. The results of my investigation, and why this is relevant to our story, are described in Appendix 5.

The detail in Appendix 5 reveals that the sizeable legacy included ongoing income rights from Norfolk properties. As we shall see, Barnabas Mayston would soon outlive his only adult sibling and possible co-legatee Mary Patten Bond. It seems clear that the legacy and the property income enabled him to set up and sustain his medical practice and comfortable family premises in Leyton and elsewhere. This in turn enabled his children, including Zoë, to benefit from educational and social opportunities which at the time would only have been accessible by those with financial means or inherited wealth.

The close link of Barnabas the elder with Rev. John Mills, as mentioned a Fellow of Cambridge University, may also have been a factor in Barnabas Mayston's choice of further medical studies at that institution later in the 1890s. The Bonds of these generations were resourceful, it would seem, and knew how to make the most of their connections.

Barnabas Mayston Bond's rural origins

Looking now at Barnabas Mayston Bond, Zoë's father, as one of the new wave of inhabitants to late Victorian Leyton, we could certainly consider him also as part of the great influx from the countryside, as described by historians: see earlier citation in End Note 9. His 1861 birth into a Norfolk farming dynasty and, as described earlier, his life at Alburgh until at least the age of ten provided an essentially rural boyhood. He had been christened at All Saints Church, Alburgh (Fig. 5) on 22 August 1861. A fourteenth-century church with nineteenth-century restorations, this ancient structure, according to the 1883 White's *History, Gazetteer and Directory of Norfolk*, has two windows in the chancel with stained glass images in memory of "the late Mr Barnabas Bond and a son of the Rector". This Bond name may refer to either the father or grandfather of Barnabas Mayston, a fact that remains to be researched and clarified.

In 1854 this village of Alburgh had 575 souls,[23] some of whom were descended from a long line of farmers named Bond, several of them also bearing the distinctive 'Barnabas' as a first name. The earliest such ancestor recorded was the Barnabas Bond who lived there from 1741 to 1814.[24] Barnabas Mayston's father Barnabas the elder, who had been encumbered with the legacy of Rev. John Wills as described earlier, farmed significant amounts of land in this area of Norfolk and employed farmhands and boys.[25] [26]

Fig. 5: All Saints Church, Alburgh, Norfolk. Photograph by Sophie Yeomans.[22]

Barnabas Mayston: marriage

Moving our attention now to his young adulthood in London, we find that on 10 July 1888, after qualifying in medicine and surgery, Barnabas Mayston Bond married Eliza Josephine Luxon at St Sepulchre, City of London.[27] This was only nine months after his mother Rebecca Ann had died. Both Eliza Josephine and Barnabas Mayston had rural backgrounds, but were from completely different parts of England. The circumstances of their meeting are not known.

Eliza Josephine's origins were in a picturesque stone-built village on the north coast of Cornwall.[28] In 1861 she had been living with her mother, also Eliza, and father George Luxon, a police sergeant, at Church Lane,[29] Padstow. They were adherents of Methodism.[30] The date of the Luxon family move to London is not known, but by the time of the marriage, Barnabas Mayston's father-in-law George Luxon's new occupation was that of surveyor.[31] It seems that Eliza Josephine also came from a family with ambition.

Chapter One

Dr Bond's residence and practice at 9 Manor Road, Leyton, Essex

From the Medical Register of 1888 noted earlier we are aware that Dr Bond had registered his practice here, but the census of 1891 contains the first recorded information of the names of Bond family members who were resident at "Treyarnon", Manor Road, Leyton, Essex. At the time the family comprised Dr Barnabas Bond, his wife Eliza Bond (née Luxon), his widowed mother-in-law Eliza Luxon (née Tremain), the two children Walter and Elsie, and a servant Rosa Humphreys who had been born in Lambeth. The house name "Treyarnon" harks back to Eliza's birthplace in Cornwall.

See Fig. 27 for a contemporary image of the substantial double-bayed double-fronted end-of-terrace house which, according to plans seen seventy years later, comprised four reception rooms, a consulting/treatment room, a scullery downstairs, six bedrooms upstairs, and an extensive cellar. It provided the Bonds with a good twelve years of raising their family.

The street plans[32] (see Fig. 6) show that the first four terraced houses in Manor Road were separated from the double-width No. 9 by an entrance-way leading to the mews at the back. They were positioned on the south-west side of the narrow entrance-way whereas the double-width No. 9 was on the north-western side.

House numbering is annotated in Fig. 6 as was extant until 1970. This part of Manor Road was completed in the late 1880s, but the parallel Lea Hall Road (visible in Fig. 6 only as 'Hall Road') was developed about ten years later. Park Road is said to mark the earlier boundary with the Leyton Grange Estate of the eighteenth century. See End Notes 310 – 313 for further background and potential enquiry.

In the 1891 census listing of Manor Road, many of the houses were identified by name rather than number, one exception being the household listed as adjacent to the Bonds and given as No. 5, where a chemist, Mr Spiers, and family lived. See Appendix 3D for further detail on house numbering of the time in this part of Manor Road.

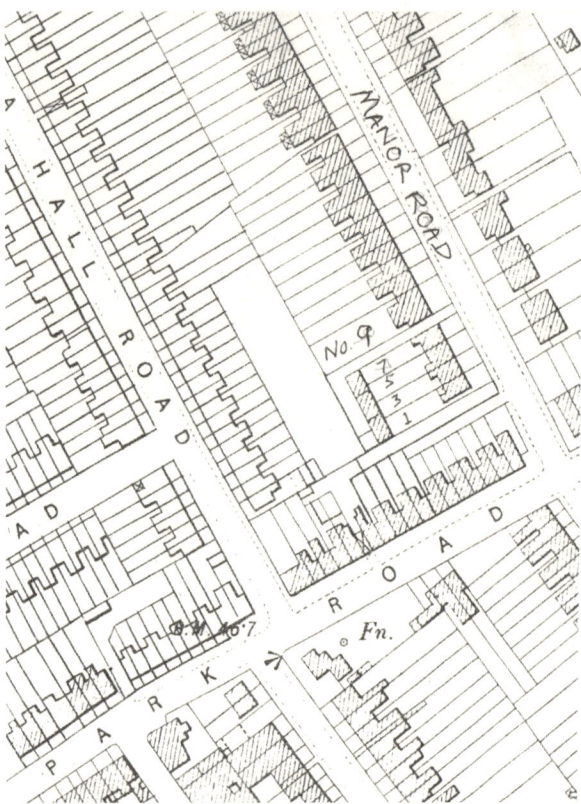

Fig. 6: *Fragment of Leyton, Essex, from Ordnance Survey.*
Courtesy of Waltham Forest Archives.

I gained no clarification on the house-numbering quandary from Millicent Zoë's autobiography as, disappointingly, she makes no mention at all of her Leyton origins: her earliest memory is that of being a four-year-old child living in Dorset.[33]

Chapter One

The Bonds' children and their baptisms

The last of five children, and the third daughter for Dr Barnabas Mayston Bond and Eliza Josephine Bond (née Luxon), Millicent Zoë was born at 9 Manor Road on 6 February 1896.

Zoë's elder siblings, bearing in mind the house-numbering inconsistency discussed above, were all born at Manor Road:

• Walter Tremayne[34] Bond born on 25 April 1889, baptised at St Saviour's Church, Walthamstow on 11 June 1889;

• Elsie Margaret Bond born on 18 September 1890, baptised at St Saviour's Church, Walthamstow on 15 November 1890

• Sylvia Christine Bond born on 9 January 1892, baptised at St Saviour's Church, Walthamstow on 20 April 1892;

• Hugh Trevor Bond, born on 13 January 1894, died at 9 Manor Road, aged 1, on 21st January 1895.

St Saviour's in Walthamstow (see Fig. 7), where the three eldest Bond children were taken to be baptised, had been built only fifteen or so years previously in 1873 – 74.[35] It was, and remains, High Anglican in tradition, which contrasts somewhat with the non-conformist parentage of the Cornish Luxons, and perhaps also with the low-church East Anglian parish background of the Bond family.[36]

Fig. 7: St Saviour's Church, Walthamstow, 2017.
Photo by author.

Fig. 8: All Saints Church and schoolyard, Capworth Street Leyton. 1893 – 1970.[37] *Image supplied by History in Pictures.*

Noticing this difference, I therefore began to look for other possible explanations as to why the first three Bond offspring were baptised at St Saviour's on the Walthamstow, northern, side of Lea Bridge Road, rather than at the nearer All Saints in Capworth Street, Leyton, in whose parish 9 Manor Road was actually located.

I discovered that during the rapid residential development of Leyton and Walthamstow, the spiritual needs of the waves of incoming residents were gradually being accommodated by the provision of additional churches and by the expansion of ecclesiastical governance. Even though an All Saints Church had already been built in Capworth Street in 1865 (designed by William Wigginton[38]) it was already failing to meet the needs of the increased population and so a further enlargement was planned. A new ecclesiastical district of All Saints was created from parts of Leyton and Walthamstow in 1886, and the second All Saints building was completed in 1893 (see Fig. 8). It accommodated 600 persons, indicating the increase in the local population.[39] Schools followed a similar pattern of growth. I surmise that this All Saints Church must have been under construction during the years 1889 – 1892, since its completion date has been documented as 1893.[40] Perhaps this could have been the reason for the Bonds to cross the Lea Bridge Road for their spiritual needs, not least the baptism of their first three offspring. This supposition has since been supported by the discovery of entries for other families with Manor Road and Capworth Street addresses in the St Saviour's baptismal records of those years.[41]

Chapter One

As for the Bond children born after the completion of the All Saints Church, no baptism record for either of them is to be found, whether in the parish records of St Saviour's, Walthamstow, or the Leyton churches of St Mary's and of All Saints. An internet search of UK records yielded no results. I conclude that Hugh Trevor, the fourth child who died in infancy, and Millicent Zoë, the youngest Bond child, were both apparently unbaptised.

The death of an infant

The cause of death of the Bonds' infant son Hugh Trevor was recorded as "Diphtheria (tracheotomy) Convulsions", by A. F. Peskett LSA MRCS. According to this record Barnabas Mayston had been present at his son's death and he was the informant.[42] Performing a tracheotomy was a known treatment for this disease at the time.[43] The assumption I make is that the operation was carried out at Dr Bond's surgery at Manor Road. Further research has shown that Dr Peskett was a locally-born medical practitioner who was resident in Leyton High Road,[44] and he was, or at some point would become, the Public Health Officer for Leyton.[45]

This tragic death in the family and the circumstances involved would undoubtedly have had particularly poignant impact on Dr and Mrs Bond, given Barnabas's professional and academic interest in public health, as will be explored in the next chapter.

Chapter Two: the Bonds move on

Barnabas Mayston Bond's further medical training

During his years in Leyton, Dr Bond, already a physician and surgeon, obtained an additional medical degree, that of Diploma of Public Health (DPH), Cambridge, 1894.[46] As we have noted, Barnabas Mayston's father, Barnabas the elder, had been associated with Rev. John Mills, a Fellow of Cambridge University. This and his continued East Anglian connections could have been the background to Barnabas Mayston's choice for his second degree, given that his first degrees had been taken in London.

The DPH had been introduced in 1875 in response to the Public Health Act of that year. This Act prompted the employment of Medical Officers of Health.[47] The DPH requirements were for a one-year (or more) qualified physician or surgeon to take six months' practical instruction followed by six months' public health work.

While preparing for the qualification, Barnabas's journey to Cambridge might possibly have included a walk along Park Road and Marsh Lane, turning north to reach Lea Bridge Station built in 1840, (see Fig. 9) and conveniently (for him perhaps) situated on the London - Cambridge Line.

Fig. 9: Lea Bridge Station in Dr Bond's time.[48]
Courtesy of Vestry House Museum,
London Borough of Waltham Forest.

Evidence of work in a hospital for infectious diseases was needed to complete the qualification.[49] There is no information as to where Barnabas Bond undertook such practical experience, but the nearest such institution to Leyton was the Eastern Fever Hospital at Homerton Grove E9,[50] which had been set up in 1883 and was augmented to cope with smallpox and scarlet fever epidemics that claimed hundreds of lives in neighbouring Hackney in the 1880s and 1890s. These were hectic and developmental times in both the prevention and the treatment of fatal diseases in densely populated areas.

While the scientific discovery of inoculation had taken place in a previous century, the using of mass vaccination as public policy yielded hazards, and the study of this would likely have constituted part of Dr Bond's Cambridge curriculum.

Dr Bond's eventual success and promotion to this new profession in public health would soon see the family moving away. We find that by 1899[51] the Bond family had transferred from Leyton to the older-established town and port of Poole in Dorset, with the newly well-qualified Dr Bond assuming there the title of Port Medical Officer of Health.

The Bonds at Poole

The 1901 census shows that the family in Poole included both the third child, Sylvia Christine, and Millicent Zoë herself (whose name was recorded in it as "Zoe M": note the change of name order which remained for the rest of her life). Zoë's autobiography refers to her age as being four when the family lived in the "old rambling house in Dorsetshire".[52]

The family's moves can also be traced (see Appendix 5) by reference to Barnabas Mayston's 'Ownership Voter' status listed in the annual Norfolk Register of Electors,[53] where his possession of 'copyholder cottages' or 'copyholder houses'[54] qualified him for this continued status. In the 1897, 1898 and 1899 Norfolk electoral registers Dr Bond's actual place of abode is given as 7 Manor Road, Leyton, (sometimes 'Leighton') Essex. In the 1900 and 1902 registers it appears as 100 High Street, Poole. The register in 1903 records another residence at Westwood, Longfleet, Poole, this being the home location most often referred to by Zoë in her book.

The censuses, although less frequent than the electoral registers, give fuller information as to the other members of the family. So we can read that there were additionally in the Bond household at Poole in the 1901 census, two retired Church of England clergymen from the Midlands, who were widowers, designated 'boarders'; a cook, a house-maid and a parlour-maid listed as domestic servants, all from Dorset.

Dr Bond's widowed mother-in-law Eliza Luxon (née Tremain) was not recorded as present with the family on 1901 census night, as she had been in the 1891 census. Furthermore, I have not been able to find records of her living elsewhere after the

Fig. 10: 30 Brook Green, Hammersmith, W6.
Dr Bond's medical premises and family residence 1907 – 1920.
Photo by author, 2017.

1891 census. Zoë's autobiography makes no mention of her Grandmother Luxon nor, incidentally, of any of the maternal Cornish heritage. However, the address recorded for Eliza Luxon's death, on 21 February 1913,[55] was Dr Bond's house and medical premises in Hammersmith. It appears therefore that she had indeed made a move at some point to west London.

From Poole to Hammersmith

The exact date of the family move to Hammersmith in west London is unknown, but would have been about eight years following their first move from Leyton to Poole.[56] 30 Brook Green, Hammersmith, London W6 is an elegant terraced villa, now showing some evidence of redevelopment since the Edwardian times. Zoë remarks[57] that this house was smaller than their home in Poole, and that alterations and additions had to be made.

Fig. 10 illustrates that No. 30 now forms one building with the next-door No. 29.[58] Note from this (contemporary) photograph that a 'School' warning sign is outside the property: this refers to the St Paul's Girls' School, situated at the end of the terrace, which institution was attended by the Bond daughters. See Chapter Four, Fig. 12.

Chapter Two

Dr Bond's work in India

While the female family members and the children possibly may have remained in Poole until as late as 1907, it becomes apparent that prior to this Barnabas was undertaking urgent medical relief work abroad. Zoë made no mention of this in her book, and cites only her father's intentions concerning the children's education as the motive for the onward move from Poole to London.

The evidence for Barnabas Mayston's overseas service turns up in the records of the Freemasons. Barnabas Mayston Bond remained a member of the United Grand Lodge of England in Norfolk,[59] even though he had long departed his East Anglian birthplace and ancestral home. Finding his registration record at the Norfolk Lodge in 1905 was not a big surprise though, and indicated that he had indeed inherited the ongoing 'Out Voter' electoral status on account of owning 'copyholder cottages/houses' held in the Norfolk parish of Pulham St Mary the Virgin,[60] as expounded in the account of *Porter v Bond*, 1873 at Appendix 5.

However the surprise was to find that in 1903, listed as a Physician Surgeon aged 44, Dr Bond had become a member of the 'Devon' Masonic Lodge in Jullundur [now known as Jalandhar], and was recorded as resident in Jullundur, Punjab. He paid up a final 7s.6d. (35p) registration fee in 1907 relating to that location, although there is no specific evidence of his whereabouts during 1903 to 1907, nor is there any date of return to England.

Although I could find no record in the UK Passenger Lists of journeys to and from the sub-continent that would confirm Dr Bond's travels, it is possible that the journeys to and from Punjab would have been under the auspices of governmental military services. By way of final corroboration of his work in the Indian sub-continent however I did find, in the last public professional record of 1935 relating to him the following announcement:

> "Bond Barnabas Mayston. Recently deceased. MRCS Eng. LRCP Lond 1886. DPH Camb 1894. St Bart. Punjab Government Inoculator, Plague 1902 – 03."[61]

I surmise that Dr Bond did indeed spend a period in India in the early 1900s and was involved in emergency medical work during the disastrous plague epidemic in the British-ruled Punjab. Half a million Punjabi villagers were inoculated in 1902 – 1903.[62]

Barnabas Mayston's Cambridge University public health qualifications and experience at the port of Poole would likely have given him expert status. Nevertheless I have not been able to find any reference to experience at St Bartholomew's Hospital, as mentioned in the Medical Register obituary cited above.

Barnabas Mayston's sister Mary 1858 – 1908

Some years after his return from Punjab, Barnabas was faced with the death of his 50-year-old single sister, Mary Patten Bond, who was briefly referred to in Chapter One. Mary herself had been aged only 19 or 20 when their mother, Rebecca Ann, already widowed, had died, but we learn from the census records that Mary Patten had been able to live on her own means in Devon[63] and later in North Kensington. 'Living on own means' is the official status whereby the censuses, in this case in 1891[64] and 1901,[65] had identified her as a 'Visitor' in the places that nevertheless were her home. This definition, as used at that time in censuses, indicated the absence of any familial, marital or employment relationship to the Head of Household. It is likely that Mary Patten's financial sustenance would have been derived directly, or indirectly via Barnabas Mayston, from the funds of Barnabas Bond the elder's legacy (as above and described in Chapter One and at Appendix 5).

Mary Patten had moved household more than once, each time being recorded as a 'Visitor'. It is interesting to note that Mary's status as a single woman in the households of others at the turn of the century contrasts with the greater degree of independence in housing that her niece, Zoë, would enjoy a decade or so later during and after the First World War.

From the records we learn that Mary Patten died on 19 February 1908. She had been Barnabas Mayston's only living sibling,[66] and was resident at 21 Redcliffe Square, South Kensington, London at the time. On 2 May 1908 Barnabas gained probate for his sister's considerable estate of £1,226.3s.8d.[67][68] As noted, women were not legally capable of investing in property then: Mary Patten had inherited money but couldn't spend it on making a home for herself.

Barnabas Mayston and Eliza Josephine – the Hammersmith years

Barnabas Mayston's move to Hammersmith had represented a return to general practice after his spell as the Poole Port Medical Officer of Health and then the field work in India. The reason given for moving to London, as we heard earlier from Zoë's writing, was a desire to improve the children's educational experience.

Occupation by the Bond family at 30 Brook Green seems to have been constant from that time to the end of the second decade of the twentieth century: Dr Bond's medical registration states his residence as being at 30 Brook Green, Hammersmith, both in 1907 and 1912, and the Hammersmith & Fulham Electoral Register for 1912 shows "Bond, Barnabas Mayston" as resident at the same place.

At the same time, while I found no evidence to show that Barnabas Mayston and his family, including his mother-in-law, were absent from the country in April 1911, their names are not to be found anywhere in the census of that year. But as mentioned above, Zoë had stated that there were alterations and additions to the premises at Brook Green, and it is therefore possible that the family could have been away from home while that was being carried out.

We later find Eliza Josephine's name appearing on the list of eligible voters, registered in 1918 at the 30 Brook Green address.[69] It is not known whether her qualification to vote was in her own right as a property owner or whether it was ascribed to her marital status vis–à-vis Barnabas Mayston. The Representation of the People Act 1918 had entitled women over the age of thirty years who were property owners or married to property owners to vote.

In her book, Zoë refers to her mother's ill-health during unspecified years in west London. The penultimate medical registration for Dr Bond at Hammersmith, and indeed in the UK, was in 1920.

The years from 1911 to 1919 saw the family's life together diminishing, with Eliza Luxon's demise in 1913, Walter Tremayne joining the army and departing for Egypt on 21 April 1915[70] and then Sylvia leaving for marriage in 1918. Elsie Margaret appears to have left home before Zoë did. In Chapter Fourteen we will glance at some more details of the subsequent lives of Zoë's sisters and brother

Chapter Three: Mulberry trees and silkworms

Zoë's silkworm hobby

According to her autobiography, Zoë had first become intrigued by silkworms at the age of four, when the family lived in Dorset. She writes that she had been:

" ... blessed with a mother who understood young minds"[71]

and notes with some joy that she was allowed by the forbearing Eliza Josephine to keep silkworms[72] in a drawer outside the children's nursery door. So it is not difficult to see how the hobby took over Zoë's fancy at that age, and later.

Zoë's elder sister Elsie Margaret has also referred to the keeping of silkworms by Zoë and, by inference, herself and others in the Bond household. (See Appendix 4, extract 1, for the letter she wrote to their former school magazine). As noted earlier, Elsie Margaret had been born in 1890, so she would have spent her first ten years at the house in Manor Road, Leyton. Referring in the letter to "some of us" having kept silkworms at home, Elsie Margaret's words give a charming glimpse into the Bonds' Edwardian-period family life and describe how Zoë's enthusiasm for the silkworm hobby had been tolerated in the early years.

Unsurprisingly, it seems to have been regarded by the family as rather a messy childhood pastime. However it meant everything to Zoë. She goes on to claim, with not a trace of modesty, to have discovered on her own how to unwind their cocoons, unwittingly (she says) employing the same methods as used by the Chinese in 5000 BC.[73]

With the silkworm pastime as a central formative influence, Zoë also writes that, contrary to the norms of the time, Barnabas chose to spend good money on the education of his three daughters,[74] and she certainly appreciated it in hindsight. Barnabas Mayston's advanced ideas about women's place in society and his desire that Zoë should develop a mind of her own are now legendary among her descendants.[75] And as we shall see, Barnabas Mayston's ideals were to become realised more than he might have anticipated.

The keeping of silkworms, feminism and literary references

Breeding silkworms at home and harvesting their produce had become a recognised pastime for middle- and upper-class children in the nineteenth and early twentieth centuries. Silkworms are not native to the British Isles and intensive sericulture over thousands of years across the globe had by then resulted in the silkworm no longer existing in the wild. The silkworm eggs were thereby the main commodities for sale that sustained this hobby. Rarely were any significant amounts of raw silk yarn obtained by amateurs.

Fig. 11: Preserved mulberry sprig from 1913, included in Rosa Luxemburg Herbarium, *Karl Dietz, Berlin, 2016.*[77]

At the same time, biology and botany, alone of the sciences, were becoming acceptable as academic pursuits for women in Britain and elsewhere. Individuals as diverse and distant as Lady Dorothy Nevill[76] and Rosa Luxemburg[77] counted among the women students of the subjects, Lady Dorothy also being involved in the silkworm breeding activity.

Virginia Woolf notably writes the hobby into the novel *Night and Day*,[78] with the character Cassandra Otway defying her disgusted mother Katharine by raising silkworms in her bedroom. It all points to a kind of cult or niche activity, so it's not unexpected that the Bond daughters of the same era were attracted to it.

A batch of silk-moth eggs in a little box, as described in the literature of the time, was given to the infant Zoë by a boy named Vincent.[79] The enlightened Dr Bond, who as discussed above may have been anxious to encourage an interest in science among his daughters,[80] may well have approved of the gift given the existence of the mulberry tree in his garden.

While appreciating Zoë's praise of her mother's tolerance, mentioned earlier, I did wonder if Eliza Josephine Bond might not have shared her daughters' enthusiasm for the messy and smelly pastime, whether at Manor Road, at Poole or in Hammersmith, and whether Zoë's continued interest in it to her teenage years could have formed part of the disaffection that would take place between Zoë and her mother.

This led me to glance briefly at the literary discussions on silkworm breeding. The lepidopteran references in Virginia Woolf's works are well-rehearsed, firstly in the development of feminism and women's involvement in science, as mentioned earlier, and secondly in the allegory of the silk-moth's sacrifice of death in order for silk to be obtained. Bringing this symbolism right up to date, in Robert Galbraith's 2014 novel *The Silkworm*[81] the moth's fate is portrayed as:

> " … a metaphor for the writer who has to go through agonies to get at the good stuff."[82]

Zoë, unsurprisingly, gives no indication that she ever had any sympathy for the silk-moths' suffering when she had them 'stifled,'[83] nor are there any clues that she went through too much agony in writing her book. Prioritising the end over the means, Zoë cheerfully expected that both the local baker and her own household cook would each permit the extermination of silk chrysalides in their ovens in order for Zoë to obtain cocoons undamaged by emerging live silk-moths.

Later we will see that at the end of her life, Zoë's remaining stock of silk lepidopterans were, perhaps somewhat resonantly, transferred to a butterfly farm where they were to continue their productive existences alongside their creature cousins for some time.

Chapter Three

The mulberry tree at 9 Manor Road, Leyton

The Manor Road mulberry (see Fig. 27) was situated at the far end (western edge) of the back garden in Manor Road. Although its precise age was not known at the time of my residence there from 1971 - 1981, it stood until 1982. At that time Barnardos, having purchased the property from me and the co-inhabitants in 1981, decided to have it felled, even though this well-known charity had been informed by me of its arboricultural value. This was a regrettable loss to the local environment and to local history.

In this account of the first occupants of 9 Manor Road, I have assumed as stated earlier that the pictured mulberry tree existed well before the urbanisation of the area. However, my attempts to verify this beyond any doubt have had limited results, as described in Appendix 3E.

While resident at 9 Manor Road I had sought the advice of the Royal Horticultural Society (RHS) at Wisley, Surrey, about caring for the mulberry tree. A reply came from H. A. Baker, Fruit Officer for the RHS dated 22 August 1975, in which he described how to cut out the dead wood and advised that a drooping branch should be supported. He cautioned against lopping the top and commented:

> "A mature mulberry usually needs very little pruning, only sufficient to keep it shapely. It is inclined to develop a rather rugged, contorted, spreading appearance which is an attractive feature of the tree." (Fig. 29[84])

This indeed had been my concern as to the robustness of the tree, as it had a long low branch extending sideways, closely resembling the Buxton House, Leytonstone specimen in Fig. 3. Having been assured by the RHS that it would respond, I duly looked after the Manor Road mulberry for the following six years until moving away, and was rewarded amply with pound upon pound of fruit which was turned into endless jams, conserves, puddings and even wine. I recall that it was not necessary to pick the fruit by hand: the easiest harvesting method was to place a sheet underneath the spreading boughs and wait for the inch-long dark red berries to drop onto it.

Chapter Four: Zoë's youth

Zoë's education: Zoë becomes a 'Paulina'

Let's now catch up with Zoë's progress at school. Following the family's second move – from Dorset to west London – her two elder sisters were taken out of their boarding school and began to attend the newly-established St Paul's Girls' School[85] at Brook Green, Hammersmith, situated two minutes away from the Bond's family home.[86]

Fig. 12: St Paul's Girls' School, Brook Green, Hammersmith.
Author's photo, 2017, shows the proximity of the school to the terrace of villas, the fourth one of which is the Bonds': No. 30.

Zoë herself would enter this school in due course; meanwhile she was sent to a primary school, also in Brook Green. Her brother Tremayne[87] attended the original St Paul's School (for boys), some of whose staff were shared with the (new) Girls' School, including one Gustav Holst. Zoë recounts somewhat tongue-in-cheek, that when she finally got to the Girls' School, this eminent composer's music lessons, despite his "unending patience"[88] were beyond her.

Appendix 4 contains extracts from *Paulina*, the journal of St Paul's Girls' School alumnae, about Zoë's life, specially curated for this book by the School Archivist. Zoë's time as a 'Paulina' is confirmed as lasting from May 1908 to July 1913, when she was between 12 and 17 years old. As referred to in Appendix 4 Zoë made full use of the school's mulberry tree to feed her silkworms in the season. Disappointingly, the tree no longer survives there. According to the School Archivist, it was possibly felled to make way for the building of the Science Wing in 1933.

An eminent and academically-focussed school from its beginnings, St Paul's Girls' was clearly the place – for those who were in a position to pay the fees – to send a daughter as preparation for university; possibly this was what Barnabas Mayston had hoped. At the school during those years Zoë was rubbing shoulders with future scientists, writers and sportswomen including novelist Angela Thirkell (1890 –1961); world-class tennis and badminton champion Kitty McKane Godfree (1896 – 1992); composer Jane Joseph (1894 – 1929); biologist Sidnie Manton (1902 – 79); astrophysicist Cecilia Payne Gaposchin (1900 – 79) and writer Dodie Smith (1895 – 1990).[89]

Although we have little information about Zoë's time at the school – there is no record of her having passed the matriculation exam for instance – her scholarly shortcomings did not seem to have disadvantaged her and as we will see later she used to her benefit the social and cultural capital of mingling with the daughters of a wide range of prominent families of the time.

The French experience: a mind of her own

Zoë did not stay on to the sixth form (termed 'seventh' and 'eighth' form at St Paul's Girls) and instead, Barnabas Mayston arranged for his youngest daughter to finish her education at a non-Catholic, unorthodox and cosmopolitan school in France: the Collège des Jeunes Filles at Saumur on the River Loire.[90] Zoë's tales of life in this French institution read like an Enid Blyton novel, with herself cast as a kind of naughtiest girl in the school.[91]

On accessing the college's own history, compiled by Joseph-Henri Denécheau, I could imagine how its continental, avant-garde character might have critically influenced Zoë's teenage years.

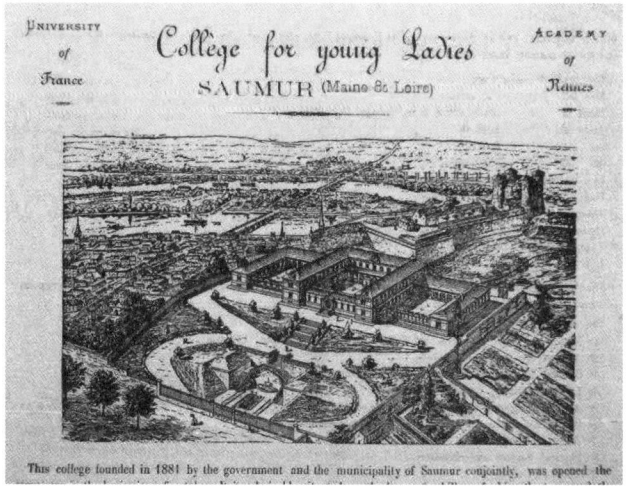

Fig. 13: Saumur Collège brochure in English c. 1905
Courtesy of the Saumur-Jadis website.

Fig. 14: *The fourth and fifth year girls at Saumur in 1914. It is likely that one of them could be Zoë. Courtesy of the Saumur-Jadis website.*

I discovered that, to attract girls from Britain, the college brochure, adorned with a fine engraving by J. Touzard and translated into English (see Fig. 13), included the emphasis that the headmistress and several professors were Protestant.

A further photograph (not reproduced here) shows the staff of the college with some sixth year pupils who undertook supervised teaching, and these young women are sporting 'la cravate ou le noeud papillon des féministes' – a floppy bow tie, elsewhere cited[92] as the badge of support for votes for women in France. Denécheau comments that many former students led an independent professional life, and that feminine emancipation was one of the aims of the establishment.

Whether Barnabas Mayston and Eliza Josephine fully appreciated and supported both the feminist and Protestant ethos of the Collège des Jeunes Filles is not known. But this choice does fit in with Barnabas Mayston's reputed enlightened ideas and the desire that Zoë would learn to develop a mind of her own.

Zoë's classmates at Saumur included girls from Russia, Germany, Austria, Spain and The Netherlands, in addition to compatriots from the British Isles.[93] Zoë initially found herself relegated to a primary age-group class due to her poor grasp of the French language. By way of consolation, she reported, the drink supplied at dinner was local wine and, as an 'étrangère', she had a private room.

Even more to her delight, by enjoining others, Zoë was able to work out novel ways of feeding her silkworms on riskily-obtained mulberry leaves. She had taken batches of eggs with her from London, kept them in her room and even, perilously, she reports, incubated them with the warmth of her body until the larvae hatched. Acquiring the mulberry leaves had included climbing out of the window at night for a clandestine rendez-vous with a would-be suitor of another girl (see End Note 91).

She became adept at subverting the school rules in order to support her silkworms. Girls were not allowed to keep pets, so she carried on in secret and in the five-week silkworm season "led a double life."[94]

The antics apart, for Zoë, this kind of 'finishing school' may have been more of a starting school, in the sense that she was exposed to a broader range of cultures and attitudes than existed at the very British St Paul's Girls' School. Having her own room because she was a foreigner, drinking wine at dinner, and mixing with French feminists surely gave her sense of ambition a significant boost.

Zoë was not the first British pupil at Saumur, but because of the outbreak of the First World War she may well have been one of the last. As early as 1893, it had been foreseen that, in the event of war, the college would be transformed into an auxiliary hospital and placed at the disposal of the Union of Women of France. Sadly, in 1914, the day school and the boarding schools were transferred to nearby buildings for this very reason. Zoë's reported gleeful activities of drainpipe climbing, mulberry tree hunting, and other mischief-making there had to come to an abrupt end, and ruefully she returned home to London after barely two years.

Back to London

In spite of the educational advantages offered by the French college, which included lessons in science and languages, Zoë apparently still had not progressed academically. She was expected by her forward-thinking parents to find a job once she was back. Unfortunately, her first attempt was not the best of choices. She writes that Barnabas Mayston's reaction to her disastrous failure in an entrance examination for employment at Barclays Bank was:

> " … to appeal to his Maker to witness that never had a man been cursed with such an imbecile for a daughter."[95]

Zoë writes in quite a matter-of-fact way about this. Nevertheless, her highlighting of the incident does suggest that it may have marked a turning point in the relationship with her father, perhaps with her mother too.

At about this time her brother Walter Tremayne had signed up for service in the First World War, and had left home for overseas service. The Bonds were left with the three teenage daughters for whom finding marriage partners was not going to be straightforward in the war years ahead and possibly any outcome was going to be costly. We will see something of this impact later.

Steps towards adult life

It seems from Zoë's writings that the Bonds did not recognise their daughter's potential for creativity and social networking as a way of advancing her chances in life. Nevertheless, we are left with an image of Barnabas Mayston, after his many years of training in medicine, surgery and public health, and his relief work in India, as a remarkably forward-thinking man of the time. It could be that the effect on Barnabas Mayston and Eliza Josephine of losing their second son so tragically in infancy may have skewed their expectations and magnified their disappointments regarding Zoë.

Barnabas Mayston was not to know that in fact he and Eliza Josephine, through their choice of schools and expectations of her independence, had given their daughter a pretty good grounding for her future life. Likewise though, the St Paul's Girls' School overlooked Zoë's lifetime achievements: Zoë's name does not yet appear in the public list of Old Paulinas (see End Note 89).

Branching out

Zoë was to spend her late teens and early twenties as a single woman enjoying life in the bohemian and cosmopolitan communities of west London, financially supported by a job in the City. Having failed to secure employment at the bank, she had taken a post in an insurance company at Cornhill.

From her writings, it seems that she adapted easily to independent life. At first, she and a friend, Madge, rented a flat. Later she moved to a room at Earls Court, rented from an unusual woman named Honeybunch, and there she also made contact with a mystery librarian referred to as 'Mr X' who was, reportedly, averse to women.[96] Zoë apparently presented no problem to him, owing to the amazing coincidence of their sharing an interest in silkworms.

Zoë reports that she celebrated the 1918 Armistice Day in style, by spontaneously running out from the crowds assembled at the Mansion House in the City of London to leap onto the back of a brewer's dray horse. The horse promptly bolted down Cheapside, with the stunningly-beautiful 22-year-old Zoë on its back,

> " … at a spanking pace urged on by the driver who was also infected by the spirit of the hour."[97]

Dr and Mrs Bond were either content with their daughter's lifestyle and pranks, or, having already decided it was better to leave Zoë to her own devices, knew little about them. In any case, Zoë writes that at some point her parents retired to the south of France[98] for reasons of her mother's ill-health.

How fortunate, in early twentieth-century terms, was Zoë that having stuck with the job of 'head cook and bottle washer'[99] for some years, she was to meet a uniquely eligible bachelor who seemingly relished her appetite for adventure and the unusual, and also came to understand her growing obsession with silkworms and their produce.

His name was Oliver Augustus Hamilton Hart Dyke.

Chapter Five: Marriage

Zoë's romance

A friend's dinner party at some point during 1920 – 21 was the occasion at which Zoë, who had been invited at the last minute, first met Oliver Augustus. In his mid-thirties, he was a mechanical engineer by profession, and was the youngest son of Sir William Hart Dyke, the 7th Baronet of Lullingstone.

Zoë and Oliver Augustus seem to have spared little time before getting married, in fact even less time than was hitherto publicly known. Noting the *Oxford Biography* (cited in End Note 3) date of 29 July 1922 for the wedding, I checked for details in the General Records Office (GRO) indexes. I was puzzled to stumble across information about another marriage, with identical participants, that had already taken place the year before on 29 July 1921. The first wedding had taken place at the Kensington Register Office, but the second was a church affair in Westminster.

In search of clarification, I looked back again at Zoë's own account: she loosely referred to their having got married "within eighteen months of meeting."[100] So I decided to probe further, in case there had been some administrative error. I applied to the GRO for the certified copies of both entries on the register.

In addition to a certified record of the publicly-reported 1922 wedding, I also received from the GRO a certified copy of the 1921 event. Both marriages were between Zoë and Oliver Augustus. While it is not unusual for couples to have both a secular and a religious wedding, in this case the two ceremonies were separated by a year, and curiously by an exact year, to the very day. The situation is partially explained, as will be explored.

I mused that perhaps the absence of a baptismal record for Zoë could have been the reason for the couple to first choose a quiet, secular ceremony, especially following what would seem to be a whirlwind romance. No members of the Bond or Hart Dyke families had been witnesses at this event. Instead, according to the records, a Myra K. Bishop and one Cecil G. Marston performed that function.

It also seems feasible that Oliver Augustus' banking on not inheriting the baronetcy[101] gave him the courage – or foolhardiness – to imagine that a wedding without the involvement of his family would not matter. What seems just as likely as any other rationale for their first wedding is that Zoë's secular, feminist education in Saumur, France (described in Chapter Four) had imbued her with modern twentieth-century notions about marriage being a civil matter. Perhaps she really did obtain that 'mind of her own' there!

From unconventional to conforming

Whatever the explanation for the register office wedding in 1921, the couple were not destined to sustain this ostensibly secretive status for long. An unexpected bereavement in the Hart Dyke family in the summer of 1922 impacted critically on the baronetcy line. This was the death of Oliver Augustus' elder brother on 27 June 1922. The second wedding between Zoë and Oliver Augustus took place very soon afterwards. The date of this second wedding was, as noted, exactly twelve months after the first one, and this time it was celebrated at St Andrew's Church,[102] Well Street, in the Parish of St Marylebone, Westminster, London.

The rank of Oliver Augustus' father, Sir William Hart Dyke, was recorded on the 1922 marriage certificate as 'Baronet', whereas on the first certificate of 1921 it had been given as 'M.P.' with no reference to the baronetcy. Sir William's career as a Member of Parliament had actually ended in 1906, although he had been the 7th Baronet since 1875. Perhaps the somewhat misleading entry of M.P. made in 1921 represented some denial or disbelief on Oliver Augustus' part about his potential position: see quotation on page 45. Life as an engineer in London may well have held more attractions for him than inheriting a country estate.

The 1922 marriage certificate shows that W. Hart Dyke (likely to be the afore-mentioned Sir William, Oliver Augustus' father) and R. P. Hart Dyke[103] formally witnessed the event. Zoë and Oliver Augustus, now aged 26 and 36 respectively, were both recorded as resident at the St Andrew's Church House the night before the wedding, not an unusual arrangement for marriages out-of-parish.

The second wedding date being precisely one year later than the first does seem to indicate that it had been arranged by the Hart Dyke family knowing that there had been a previous ceremony.

But who else knew? The name of the best man at the 1922 wedding, C. G. Marston, almost certainly is a match for the Cecil G. Marston who had been a witness at the first ceremony in 1921. To what extent any Church personnel may also have been aware that the couple were already married is not likely to be in any public record since the marriage was conducted following banns having been called. This practice ostensibly satisfies the Church about the integrity of the marriage[104] since it gives the opportunity for objections to the proposed union to be raised. Notably, on the wedding certificates at both events Zoë and Oliver Augustus were each assigned the respective statuses of 'Spinster' and 'Bachelor'.

The delicate situation was handled discreetly by the Hart Dyke family at the time as can be seen in this press notice:

> "The marriage of Mr Oliver Hart Dyke son of the Right Hon Sir William and Lady Emily Hart Dyke, and Miss Millicent Zoe Bond, daughter of Dr Mayston Bond and Mrs Bond, took place early on Saturday morning at St Andrew's Church, Wells-street, Oxford-street. The bride, who wore a dress of white

Georgette with a large white picture hat trimmed with ostrich feathers, was given away by Mr C. W. Davies. The Rev. Cyril B. Marshall, the Vicar, officiated, and Mr C. G. Marston acted as best man. The marriage was a very quiet one owing to mourning in the bridegroom's family."[105]

The Hart Dyke lineage and the second wedding

This family bereavement being mourned was, as noted above, the death of Oliver Augustus' brother Percyvall. Percyvall had married at the age of 37, incidentally at the same St Andrew's Church, Marylebone, in 1908. He died on 27 June 1922 at Bournemouth, aged only 50. Since Percyvall had no offspring to inherit the title, the sad bereavement placed Oliver Augustus in line to the baronetcy second only to his father Sir William Hart Dyke, the 7th Baronet. In the event, Sir William was to live on until 1931 giving Oliver Augustus a decade in the preparatory role.

This turn of events in June 1922, as we have noted, is the most feasible explanation for the more conventional, if speedy, church wedding of Zoë and Oliver Augustus one month later in July. With Percyvall's demise, the family line had passed unexpectedly to Oliver and this prompted an urgent need to ensure continuity for the Hart Dyke line. The previous 1921 Register Office marriage might have been considered by the Hart Dykes as inadequate in the eyes of God for titled inheritance purposes. And at the same time, given the 'fashionable society' reputation of the St Andrew's Church,[106] it is likely that there was also a social status and celebration expectation surrounding the actual wedding of the prospective incumbent of the baronetcy.

With Zoë being given away by the (unidentified) C. W. Davies rather than her father and, as will be explored later, with Dr Barnabas Mayston Bond and Eliza Josephine by then out of the country, the culminating situation is that Zoë had got married twice in the space of a year to the same bridegroom, each time without the benefit of parental support.

All public records of the Hart Dyke inheritance line state the date of Zoë and Oliver Augustus' marriage to be 29 July 1922. Prior to that date Zoë's name does not appear in any publicly-available documentation as a member of the Hart Dyke family, even though she and Oliver Augustus were legally married from 1921.

Marriages of Zoë's siblings

Before we leave the topic of weddings, there is one more curious and slightly odd factor involved. Only one day after Zoë and Oliver Augustus' first wedding, in fact on 30 July 1921, Zoë's elder sister Elsie Margaret Bond and one Ernest Percival Sterling Lomax were also standing before the very same Kensington Registrar, A.J. Turner, in a marriage ceremony of their own. Ernest, a bachelor, described as an Artist (Designer) was aged 44, and spinster Elsie was 30.[107] He had served in the First World War,[108] and at the time of the wedding they were resident at separate addresses in the Notting Hill Gate area of west London.

The quiet marriages of the two Bond sisters so close together and at the same location could paint a romantic picture of their having made the most of young adult life without parental restraints in post-First World War London. However neither of them had acted as witness for the other as might have been expected. This simply adds to the mystery. The names of witnesses at Elsie Margaret and Ernest's wedding, George and E. Schofield, provide us with no additional explanatory information other than to further illustrate that none of the three weddings held in 1921 and 1922 involving the Bond daughters were witnessed by the senior generation of the Bond family.

One explanation for the two modest register office ceremonies of the elder and younger Bond daughters could have been that no money for weddings had been set aside by Dr and Mrs Bond on their departure from Hammersmith in 1919 – 1920. They had, it would seem, made the appropriate provision for their middle daughter, Sylvia Christine, back in 1918.

Zoë's sister, who was four years her senior, and William Wilson Simpson, an electrical engineer, had wed on 7 September 1918.[109] The event was convened by licence rather than by the calling of banns, and held at the local St John the Baptist Parish Church in Holland Road, Kensington. Sylvia married from the Bond family home address, 30 Brook Green. The witnesses recorded included B. M. Bond and E. J. Bond (without doubt Barnabas Mayston and Eliza Josephine). Another witness was 'Fredk' A. Bond, an untraceable name in connection with our Bonds so perhaps was not even related.

Other than banns not having been called, the ceremony seems to have taken place in a traditional way with full Bond family involvement. The background of the First World War and its privations may be part of the explanation for the speedier licence-based ceremony.

What little has been discovered of the later marriage, overseas, of the eldest Bond offspring Walter Tremayne to Evelyn May Hardy, is noted in Chapter Fourteen.

Chapter Six: The Hart Dyke line continues

Having set up home in commuter-belt Leatherhead, Surrey, after their 'official' wedding, Zoë and Oliver Augustus duly met the family expectations: three children were born between 1924 and 1930, including two boys, thus producing future heirs.

Fig. 15: The christening of Derek Hart Dyke at Lullingstone, 1925.
Left to right: Lady Emily Caroline Hart Dyke née Montagu; the 9th Earl of Sandwich; Zoë holding Derek William Hart Dyke; Mrs Billinghurst (untraced); Oliver Augustus Hart Dyke.
Photo credit: TopFoto.

Derek William 1924 – 1987

Derek Hart Dyke, the elder son, was born on 4 December 1924. Fig. 15 shows the family group at his christening. He was to become Sir Derek William Hart Dyke, 9th Baronet, and would live until 1987.

Oliver Guy 1928 – 2018

Oliver Guy Hart Dyke[110] (known as Guy), Zoë and Oliver Augustus' second son was born to Zoë and Oliver Augustus on 9 February 1928. Oliver Guy married his distant cousin Sarah Alexander Hart Dyke, Sir Percyvall Hart Dyke the 5th Baronet having been their common ancestor. See the Hart Dyke outline ancestry diagram in Appendix 2A.

David William 1955 –

Following the death of Sir Derek William in 1987, the baronetcy passed to his son David William Hart Dyke. A grandson of Zoë and Oliver Augustus, David William had been born to Derek William and his first wife Dorothy (née Moses) in 1955. David William remains as the 10th Baronet. He currently has no direct heirs to pass the title to and he lives in Canada. Lullingstone Castle and the estate are maintained as a working estate and a place of historical and environmental interest to summer visitors by the family of the late Oliver Guy Hart Dyke.

Tom Hart Dyke 1976 –

Thomas Guy Hart Dyke, the son of Oliver Guy and Sarah Hart Dyke, is in line to inherit the baronetcy, assuming that David William, the 10th Baronet, produces no heirs in the meantime. Thomas Guy comments philosophically about this.[111] A grandson of Zoë and Oliver Augustus, Tom is the well-known botanist of TV and gardening fame and author of the autobiographical *An Englishman's Home* quoted throughout our book.

Resident at Lullingstone Castle, he has installed there the World Garden.[112] Tom's track record in botany has been recognised in an honorary doctorate from Canterbury Christ Church University, awarded on 27 January 2017.

Interestingly, elements of his educational record echo those of his Grandma Zoë, the grandmother he never knew. Having spent primary years sneaking out of school to study local wild orchids,[113] he left the school sixth form a year early and found his real educational home at Sparsholt College, a further education institution, where he studied tree surgery and forestry. At a similar stage Zoë was enjoying her two years at the college in France.

A long and terrifying period of being held in captivity in Bolivia when on a plant-discovery trip, as recounted in his autobiography, was a hugely formative influence on his life, and the creation of the World Garden at Lullingstone has been Tom's positive response to the ordeal.

Lady Emily Caroline Hart Dyke (née Montagu) 1846 – 1931

The Hart Dyke family is not without unusual characters. The formal group photograph at Fig. 15, which features Lady Emily Caroline and her father the Earl of Sandwich at the christening of Derek William, appears to reveal Lady Emily's attire as a shirt, collar and tie topped with a formal jacket and watch fob chain. However, given that she was, to Zoë's gleeful admiration, a drummer, an amateur billiard champion and a repairer and caner of the neighbourhood's chairs,[114] a possible – uncorroborated – explanation for the unusual costume is that she had been providing the musical entertainment at that family event.

Interestingly though, Lady Emily's lineage outperforms that of the Hart Dykes in terms of historical length and royal linkage, with a direct link back to the 1625-born 1st Earl of Sandwich, Edward Montagu, and an eventual link to William the Conqueror.[115]

Rosemary June Hart Dyke 1930 – 1995

Rosemary was Zoë and Oliver Augustus' only daughter. She was born on 27 January 1930 and died on 1 November 1995. Rosemary, known as June in the family, was given an additional middle name of Tremayne after her uncle (Zoë's elder brother Walter), a name that originated from the maternal Cornish ancestry.

Amanda Zoë Frances Farr 1953 –

Rosemary's daughter Amanda was born in 1953 and appears to be the only descendant yet to be blessed with the name of Barnabas Mayston Bond's youngest daughter, our central character.

Anya Hart Dyke 1978 –

A third direct descendant of Zoë and Oliver Augustus is Guy and Sarah's daughter Anya, who now has a young family of her own.

Other members of the wider Hart Dyke family

For interest, it is worth mentioning here two other publicly-known Hart Dyke personalities. Thomas Guy's cousin, Miranda Katherine Hart Dyke, born in 1972, is better known as Miranda Hart, the actor and comedian.

Miranda's father, Captain David Hart Dyke, born in 1938, is the elder brother of Sarah Alexander Hart Dyke. He went on to be the surviving commanding officer of HMS *Coventry*, a ship that sank in the Falklands War of 1982.

Chapter Seven: Zoë and Oliver's partnership

Life at Leatherhead

From the mid-1920s through to the early 1930s Zoë and Oliver Augustus were bringing up their young family in a grand detached house named The Wilderness[116] at Tyrells Wood near Leatherhead. This Home Counties secluded suburban neighbourhood compared unfavourably in Zoë's mind with her earlier offbeat and stimulating existence in cosmopolitan London. With commuters for neighbours, Zoë, like the other wives, ran the household, played golf and tennis, rode horses and went swimming, in what she calls "a gay group"[117] – a phrase that perhaps was a euphemism for circumstances that, although sociable, were superficial and boring, and from which she couldn't wait to get away.

Nevertheless, being able to afford staffed nurseries at home, Oliver Augustus and Zoë were not completely prevented from pursuing their own interests. At the same time though, Oliver's engineering pursuits confining him to home instead of being a City commuter like the other husbands in the rural outskirts of Leatherhead, began to reinforce Zoë's frustration. As will be noted later, this time was said by Zoë to herald the cooling off in their relationship. She points out ruefully that for ten years the silkworms had had to take a secondary place.[118]

Admirably though, she was using the time to learn about the science of sericulture and to discover where supplies of silkworm eggs and mulberry leaves could be bought on a more commercial scale. Her scientific knowledge about the botany of mulberries, the zoology of the *bombyx mori* (silk-moth) and the methods of obtaining raw silk were all self-taught, even to the extent of her travelling daily from Leatherhead to the Natural History Museum in London to copy in longhand 365 pages of botanical detail and instructions.[119] Dr Bond eventually might have been proud of his daughter, had he lived long enough to know of her application to study and its successful results.

A key initial challenge was the non-availability of equipment since there were no established cocoon-washing or silk-reeling machine manufacturers or even regular stockists of such in Britain. Here is where Oliver Augustus stepped in. He began to devote his skills to designing from scratch the various contraptions and structures needed for hatching the eggs, housing and feeding the silkworms, eliminating the subsequently unwanted moths, unravelling their cocoons into raw silk and completing the filature process.

Some historians claim that it was unusual for a son in the titled gentry to embrace a profession such as engineering, as Oliver Augustus had done, but research shows that he was not the first such member of the Hart Dyke family to be gifted in that way: Thomas Hart Dyke (1834 – 1906) a cousin of his father the Rt Hon William, had been a Member of the Institute of Civil Engineers.

Chapter Seven

How the partnership worked

At first, it would appear that Zoë's zany unorthodoxy had met its foil in Oliver Augustus: he seems to have been a "modest, rather self-effacing man",[120] and, from Zoë's writings, an idiosyncratic boffin with an eye for precision.[121] On meeting Zoë in his early middle-age, he had, apparently, no academic or military aims in life and, as we have seen, was not expecting to inherit the baronetcy. Oliver Augustus had seemingly married the vivacious Zoë in a whirl. Her mundane City occupation belied what was becoming an exciting and obsessive hobby, and she was by that time, maybe unusually, quite independent of parents. An ideal, if quirky, relationship perhaps ensued. But the apparently carefree, although covert, union up until the 1922 wedding had given way to domestic conventionality and hard work during the ensuing decades.

The patient Oliver Augustus was thus the primary figure who would comply with the increasing demands of Zoë's silkworm-rearing passion and its consequent physical requirements, the first phase of which was launched in the attic of the massive house in Leatherhead. We read[122] that courtesy of Oliver Augustus' construction and design skills, but also Zoë's willingness to scrub and whitewash, the silkworms eventually benefited from generously-spaced loft-style accommodation across the whole house, their converted location having caused the displacement of the children's nurseries to a newly-extended wing.

Zoë's creative and practical skills, combined with the technical support of Oliver Augustus, characterised the couple's combined strengths in designing and implementing the great sericulture endeavour. Unsurprisingly though, the very different nature and approach of each eventually put a brake on its sustainability.

Zoë's facility for getting things done

Both her own book and the account by grandson Tom (in his elsewhere quoted *An Englishman's Home,* see End Note 8) provide page after page of amazing tales of Zoë's ingenuity, non-conformity and ability to get things done or – as Tom drily remarks – to persuade others to do so.

Her standing in the middle of the railway tracks at the nearby Eynsford Station to make sure that any train, carrying contingents of the 40,000 Lullingstone visitors per annum, would actually stop to let them alight, is but one example, cited in both books.

Importing silkworm eggs from Turkey, equipment and machinery from Italy, and obtaining hundreds of mulberry plants from Palestine (using the good offices of Walter, her brother resident in supposedly-nearby Egypt) were not beyond her. Getting the town baker at Leatherhead to slaughter by 'stifling' hundreds of burgeoning cocoon-bound silk moths in the bread oven, as outlined in Chapter Three, was an even weirder example - that Zoë admits to keeping very quiet about at the time.[123]

Of the many other absurd situations recounted by Zoë, the events following her 1935 arrival by train in the north of Italy are probably the most far-fetched, although credible, and illustrate perfectly Zoë's imposing manner and impact on those around her.

Her plans to be met at Milan station by an Irish woman married to an Italian marquis had fallen through. Zoë recounts that having spent two days on the train from London for the sole purpose of visiting an Italian silk farm, she was in no mood for standing indefinitely on a station platform looking uninvited. So she beckoned a porter who obediently guided her to a hotel.

Zoë effusively reports that she was:

> " ... escorted without delay to a huge bathroom, provided with towels and everything the heart of woman could desire, and – the finishing touch – a tray bearing a bottle of wine and sandwiches was tenderly placed beside the bath: then with smiles the manager, the under-manager, the commissionaire, a waiter, the chambermaid and my porter, withdrew."[124]

One is tempted to think that Zoë may have embellished the facts here, but I do try to bear in mind what she would have gleaned from her youthful experiences at the Collège des Jeunes Filles in France.

The visit to the Italian filatures ensued successfully and Zoë returned having purchased equipment and supplies. However, none of it could be put to use due to Zoë's having failed to obtain the technical instructions. Undaunted, she wrote back to the marquis and got his agreement to host a kind of work experience for her employee, one Mrs Joseph, to learn the tricks of the trade.

Apparently Zoë was not being at all droll when she commented:

> " ... they refused to let me pay a single penny for her training."[125]

Chapter Eight: Inheritance of Lullingstone

Fig. 16: Lullingstone Castle Gatehouse (built 1497).
Water-colour sketch © Lindsay Topping.[126]

The catalyst for change: from Leatherhead to Lullingstone

Unhappily for Oliver Augustus, his father the Rt Hon Sir William Hart Dyke, 7th Baronet, had died on 3 July 1931. Although that had left him both the estate and title of 8th Baronet Dyke of Horeham, Sussex,[127] the resulting death duties, already enormous, were suddenly doubled due to Lady Emily Caroline, Sir William's widow, having died within the next five weeks.[128] Such is the English law on inheritance. Oliver Augustus was only able to meet the duties by selling off 5,000 acres of the Lullingstone estate to the Kemp Town Brewery.[129]

Seventy years later, the late Oliver Guy, his son, was to write, in terms of history being repeated:

> "My father never expected to inherit Lullingstone and neither did I. Being second sons we believed that the responsibility would never be ours "[130]

Guy further records[131] in the contemporary publicity brochure about Lullingstone that, even though his father (Oliver Augustus) had converted the house and gatehouse into apartments, the rents did not cover the high costs of maintenance at the time.

The formidable buildings and grounds at Lullingstone would have demanded significant time and effort from Oliver Augustus to maintain, and the financial challenge before him was immense. Zoë's seemingly brilliant solution had been that her amateur silk-production could be upgraded from the attic at Leatherhead to the land and buildings afforded by the newly-empty Lullingstone Castle. She persuaded her husband to fill much of the estate with mulberry bushes and the house with the silkworms and paraphernalia.

The allure of the silkworms

Zoë was without doubt completely fascinated by the silkworms from early childhood. Her interest in their lifecycle and activities, and her readiness to risk penalty in pursuit of their required nourishment, are illustrated in her own account and elsewhere. Photographs in her book and in publicity media of the time frequently show Zoë caring for the silkworms or tending the cocoons. It seems that Zoë would go to any lengths to protect these larvae, of which she had hundreds of thousands each season, right up until they had completed their task of spinning and could be discarded. The Lullingstone Castle annual service in the Hart Dyke ancestral church for the blessing of the silkworms represents what some might say is a bizarre degree to which Zoë's held the short-lived creatures in esteem.[132]

Zoë's motivations for stepping up the pace

Reflecting that the instigation for the setting up of the silk farm had been Zoë's brainchild and passion, we now see a further boost that pushed fascination into obsession. This was the novelty of using her new position to advance the commercial possibilities. She was already a go-getter, and now with a titled status there was no stopping her. Given that she had not been brought up in this milieu, she would have faced challenges in settling to a different lifestyle. Apparently she walked it, although in her wake was the young family. Zoë became a driving force in the development of the working silk farm and adored the flattery that it produced.

Zoë's ardour was not only for the operational business of housing the silkworms and getting them to produce the silk. She aspired to expert status, researching the international history and practices of sericulture. An appendix of twenty pages on the subject is in her 1949 book and her chapter on the history of silk[133] gives a globe-wide view. Quite dispassionately, (given that the Second World War had ended only four years previously) she discusses the silk industries of "Nazi Germany", Japan and Italy, and later even indicates an interest in the sericulture of the USSR citing the *Soviet News* of January 1946 and its references to birch-leaf-eating silkworms.[134] It seems to have been an all-embracing passion which in Zoë's mind eclipsed international conflicts and differences. An alternative, less kind assessment is that she knew little about geography or politics.

The move from Leatherhead to Lullingstone took some time to complete. When the silkworms were first transferred to Lullingstone, the family home itself was not moved at the same time, so Zoë commuted daily from Leatherhead by car to tend them. We will find later that Oliver Augustus was already beginning to feel dissatisfied with the situation.

The final complete move of the silkworms and their entire paraphernalia was eventually spurred on by the 1936 visit to Lullingstone of Queen Mary.

Chapter Eight

Royal patronage and cult status

The 1936 visit to Lullingstone Castle by Queen Mary, ten days prior to which Zoë had called upon Dartford Rural Council to lay the extensive driveway, and for which she had brought in villagers specially to weed the mulberry plantation, was the watershed that propelled Zoë and the silk farm into a cult status that would endure for many years. She was sought after for exhibitions and lectures both at home and abroad and travelled widely. In 1936 she was interviewed for *In Town Tonight* on BBC Radio,[135] the Science Museum asked for silk production specimens, and she was to give a lecture at the Royal Society of Arts achieving a silver medal.[136]

Fig. 17: Visit of Queen Mary to Lullingstone Silk Farm, 1936.
Deferential Zoë (floral patterned dress and large hat) accompanies Queen Mary (holding umbrella) on Thursday 25 June, 1936.
Photo credit: TopFoto. [137 138]

A Kent newspaper of the time, (see *Selected Bibliography and References 3*), dubbed Zoë's experiment "an infant industry of Kent", explaining that supplies of mulberry leaves had to be sought by public appeals in order to supplement the low production of the immature bushes at Lullingstone. Even so, the account quotes that 1,500 lbs of raw silk was reported to Queen Mary as that year's yield.

Although the royal visit was categorised as 'private', Zoë determined to make the most of the occasion. As mentioned, Oliver Augustus finally moved the silkworms' feeding trays and spinning accommodation out of the Leatherhead attic and garage. Incurring the renovation of the former laundry at Lullingstone, this was a major exercise and battle against time, as Zoë describes.

> " [the laundry] was in a very dilapidated state as it had not been used for years and the walls and windows were in a pretty hopeless condition. Nothing daunted, he [Oliver Augustus] laid down a concrete floor, installed electric light, had the window repaired and the whole place distempered and painted within a week."[139]

Queen Mary was received in the house by the enthusiastic Zoë and, presumably, an exhausted Oliver Augustus, where Her Majesty was introduced to the silkworms in their new quarters. After viewing the mulberry plantation from her limousine the Queen was bade farewell by a contingent of the Dartford Rural Fire Brigade, local nurses and village girls who were lined up on the lawn. This brilliant touch of pomp and formality, dreamed up by Zoë, not only made the Kent local press as mentioned above, but also caught the imagination of an unknown artist.[140]

Chapter Nine: The peaks of achievement

Advancing the role of women artists

Lullingstone Silk Farm, as a home-country processing and production enterprise in textiles, was an idea whose time had come. Zoë's heydays were in the latter half of the 1930s, a time when she was associating with high-profile women movers and shakers. She was involved closely with leading women artists of the day, as illustrated for instance by an invitation from Betty Joel, the furniture designer, to collaborate.

Betty Joel was:

> "... one of the small number of designers who assimilated the modern aesthetic and produced a uniquely British response to the needs of the post-war period. By 1937 she was the most revered name in bespoke furniture in England, with clients ranging from show business and professional names to industry and Royalty.[141]

Betty Joel's project was a *Coronation Exhibition*[142] to be held in the Betty Joel Galleries, 25 Knightsbridge, London SW[143] and included notable women artists of the day including Dame Laura Knight (renowned painter and graphic artist), Anna Zinkeisen (sculptor and war artist), Eileen Hunter (fabric designer), Marion Dorn (textile designer) and Zoë. At this all-woman 'George VI Period' exhibition Zoë displayed damasks and brocatelles (upholstery brocade) and participated with the other artists in giving lectures twice weekly.[144]

In terms of aesthetic reputation this marks a high spot in Zoë's career. Clearly though, Zoë was not the artistic designer of the finished objects that she exhibited: her role was to supply the processors and manufacturers with the optimum quality silk yarn with a view to its being utilised by the leading artists of the day. This highly specialised craft community was happy to take up Lullingstone silk yarn because of its origin, quality and reputation. We will look in a later chapter at other key individuals whose lives and talents touched Zoë.

Expertise in sericulture

Let's look at the words of John Martin in the *Oxford Biography*,[145] recording succinctly how Zoë's remarkable role, not forgetting that of Oliver Augustus, in pioneering the re-establishment of British sericulture, took effect:

> "... their activities rapidly became famous, and Queen Mary made an official visit to their silk farm on 25 June 1936. By this time Zoë was a leading expert on the British silk industry, organizing talks and demonstrations of the latest developments in silkworm production that were taking place at Lullingstone Castle. As a result she was awarded a silver medal by the Royal Society of Arts."

Ten years later in 1946 she had risen in reputation and expertise to become a member of the Imperial Institute Silk Advisory Committee, and served also on its Technical Sub-Committee.[146]

Gaining this highly specialist reputation was not an easy ride for our heroine. The precise purpose of what was to be a baptism of fire for her at the Royal Society for the Encouragement of Arts, Manufactures and Commerce (RSA) in November 1936 was unknown to Zoë in advance of her delivery of a lecture there.

She had been invited to the RSA meeting by Mr Goodale (later Sir Ernest Goodale), the Chairman and Managing Director of the leading textile processors Warners. This company, which specialised in silk-dyeing and weaving, particularly velvet and furnishings,[147] was to become the sole supplier to the king and queen of silk for coronations and royal weddings.[148]

It was obviously in Mr Goodale's interest that Zoë's existence as a silk producer outside the brotherhood of the mainstream silk weavers and dyers (whose output was based exclusively on imported yarn supplies) be handled carefully. He knew that they would be sceptical of her capacity to produce adequate quality raw silk for turning into royal robes, and they would fear her as a competitor in the market to supply Warners and other fabric designers. The political imperative of accessing British-made silk yarn would be of great business advantage to Warners, they would know.

Zoë's own account[149] of the RSA's meeting on 25 November 1936 is more concise than the official record.[150] The RSA *Journal* (see *Selected Bibliography and References 2*) reproduces Zoë's delivered lecture in full, amounting to nine pages. Zoë more simply records that:

> "I found myself on a lonely platform, facing a large audience... Mr Goodale then gave me an encouraging smile and sat down, and I began my lecture. After I had finished he opened the discussion. I was asked many questions. After I had answered them to the best of my ability the meeting terminated."

In the RSA *Journal* there are also four pages devoted to a record of the item "Discussion" that followed Zoë's lecture. A pointed question came from a member, Mr H. Solman, who opened up the matter of British sericulture economics:

> "I suppose it would not be kind to pour cold water on Lady Hart Dyke's courageous venture, but at what price per pound does she expect to be able to produce silk in England ... I am afraid the answer is going to be very much in excess of any foreign price..... I do think that it is perhaps a kindness to tell Lady Hart Dyke that however much we might like to buy her silk and use it, we unfortunately have to consider the price, because if we don't our foreign competitors will."

Chapter Nine

Zoë was familiar with the argument: she elsewhere refers to telling the RSA about the government's imposition of sanctions against the fascist government of Italy in 1934 which had incurred the immediate loss of 400,000 silkworms at Lullingstone. Explaining just how critical the importing of mulberry plants was to the silk farm, she had told the RSA audience:

> "I tried every honest and dishonest means to get the bushes into this country." [151] [152]

One benevolent interpretation of her officially-recorded remarks might be that Zoë was blessed with a keen sense of satire. But such subtlety doesn't seem to be one of her attributes at all. I suspect that she simply favoured the ends justifying her means. Mr Goodale from the Chair smoothed over the tensions bubbling in the meeting, giving a discreet summing up in which he commented, perhaps somewhat cynically:

> "Lady Hart Dyke has, as you will have seen, a wonderful gift of imparting her enthusiasm to others, and she is fortunate in having such a powerful ally in her husband, Sir Oliver."

Oliver Augustus' qualities have been described, as we have seen, variously as patient and compliant, modest and self-effacing, giving us the picture of a backroom person involved in nitty-gritty of the estate finances and the silk filature machinery. A description by Mr Goodale of him as 'powerful' does not accord with that and comes over as rather a gratuitous bit of name-dropping.

While Zoë seemed to be out of her comfort zone here, with the sceptical textile manufacturers and businessmen, she does appear to have been a novel kind of protégée for Ernest Goodale. Utilising the supplies from Lullingstone Silk Farm had marked the first time in Warners' long history that they could offer high-quality silk fabric sourced from Britain.

Subsequently Mr Goodale was to broker all Zoë's orders for the royal occasions. In order to establish her credentials, given that she had no academic or practical qualifications, had not served an apprenticeship, and what's more was a woman, an appearance before the 'baying wolves' was a necessary pre-requisite before awarding her the RSA silver medal.[153] Such a recipient however fitted well with the RSA's role and Zoë basked in the award albeit alongside four other recipients. She was indeed a leading expert in Britain on the art, science and technology of silk.

Supplying silk for royal occasions

The visit of Queen Mary to Lullingstone and the connection with Warners and the RSA culminated in Zoë's first pinnacle of success as a supplier to the sovereign: the furnishing of silk for the coronation of King George VI. The next major occasion was the wedding of future monarch Princess Elizabeth and Philip Mountbatten on 20 November 1947.

On occasions Zoë had to import bulk amounts of silkworm eggs from China to fulfil the royal occasion orders in the time required, and a later newspaper article about the wedding explained:[154]

> "Norman Hartnell, the dress's designer, had been forced to refute vicious rumours that the dress had been woven by 'enemy' silk worms from Japan and Italy. In fact the silk was woven at Lullingstone castle in Kent using politically acceptable Chinese worms."

As we will see in Chapter Twelve, coronation robes and wedding dresses were made with Lullingstone silk through to the 1980s.

Zoë's achievements: Hart Dyke family members' views

Together with members of the Leyton & Leytonstone Historical Society, I made a visit to Lullingstone in the summer of 2017. Regular conducted tours of the house at Lullingstone Castle have always included tales of the silk farm; visitors are told by the expert guide that there are even some members of the public who still recall it.

In the Queen Anne room a chest that contains silk cocoons and skeins of silk yarn are pointed out together with relevant photographs. A framed print of the image of Zoë with Queen Mary (as seen at Fig. 17) takes pride of place on the grand piano in the drawing room. But upstairs, the guide suggests gently to the assembled sightseers that some of the former Lady Hart Dyke's activities "have had a veil drawn over them".

Hoping to find out more about how Zoë's drive to succeed might have affected the way that she is now portrayed at Lullingstone, I spoke with members of Zoë's surviving family and also glimpsed at press reports and other papers, by kind permission of Guy and Sarah Hart Dyke.[155] Zoë's pioneering activity is seen by them to have been at a great cost to the family of the time.

I had also read the comments of Zoë's grandson Tom (who was born just after Zoë died) on how certain aspects of her personality and activities tellingly come over in her autobiography *So Spins the Silkworm*. Scathingly, he comments that there is "little sign of tender emotion" in respect of her children, pointing out that Zoë refers, in the book, to her immediate family members only by their relationship, not their name. He adds the throwaway line:

> " ... she was not what you would have called a mumsy kind of mum."[156]

Chapter Nine

Talking this over with the late Oliver Guy, Zoë's younger son I probed further. He was critical of the childhood he had experienced at her hands, indicating politely that motherhood had not been her forte.

Anya, Oliver Guy's daughter, when interviewed elsewhere, was reported as having a more positive, perhaps sympathetically feminine, picture of Zoë's legacy, even though she would not have known her grandmother:

> "I so admire that she put everything she had into the silk farm... It's amazing when you think of it — it's a real achievement and it was all started as a hobby!" [157]

Tom's comments add to Anya's assessment:[158]

> "Granddad Oliver was a mechanical engineer by training ... Quite apart from the financial acrobatics he had to perform so that the Hart Dykes could remain in at least part of the estate, he had another huge challenge in life: trying to keep pace with his first wife Zoë."

Listening to more comments from Guy and his wife Sarah Hart Dyke, I heard that the unpredictable financial side of the silk farm caused untold repercussions and were resolved only by Zoë pressing others to get things done through or by some unconventional direct action.

A commentator in a national newspaper observed at the time:[159]

> "Zoe Lady Hart-Dyke is a vivid, charming woman with enough restless energy to drive the Flying Scotsman. *'Going to start a country club in the Queen Anne room here'* she explained with a hearty laugh... We hurtled round her pretty cottage. *'My daughter sleeps up there when she's home.'* She pointed to a hole high in the wall. *'She has to climb in via the bookcase.'*" [160]

So it was ever thus. Zoë's climbing escapades at the French college in order to obtain silkworm eggs were perhaps only the start of a lifetime of bending rules and inveigling others to connive in order to reach her own goals. As grandson Tom comments:

> "I imagine Zoë could have got away with murder in the mulberry bushes if she wanted to."[161]

Chapter Ten: Zoë's challenges

Business sense

While Zoë excelled at meeting and influencing the appropriate people, her entrepreneurship had its limits: Zoë appeared to pay little attention to finances. She discovered in 1933 that she was selling silk yarn at ten shillings (50p) per pound when it had cost her forty-eight shillings and sixpence (£2.45) to produce it.[162]

Making profits from the business, although a quoted overall aim, did not appear to critically govern or temper Zoë's approach. But by 1935, as can be seen from the letter written by Zoë's sister Elsie Margaret (see Appendix 4, extract 1) although the botanical, agricultural and mechanical issues at Lullingstone were well under way, those financial and economic challenges of the experiment in sericulture were looming.

Elsie Margaret's letter had gone on to state:

> "The main object of her [Zoë's] work in these experiments is to discover whether it be possible to revive and maintain silkworm culture as a paying commercial proposition in the Home Country."

Zoë's hugely ambitious life project was thus not just about growing mulberries, breeding silkworms and spinning the silk, it was about running the whole thing as a large-scale profitable enterprise within the United Kingdom. No-one else had done that, not even the Huguenots in Spitalfields.[163] She had turned her mind to this from 1933, and the extent and complexity of such an ambition was to fill the rest of her life and engulf that of others, perhaps whether they wanted it or not.

Investments

The economics of commercial raw silk production at Lullingstone were wildly ambitious, and it's clear from Zoë's writings that she was almost recklessly unaware of this. To devote twenty-one acres to a crop of mulberry bushes whose spring and summer leaves would nourish just one season's hatchings of silkworms was the first investment needed. Such intensive plantation development required knowhow and a workforce to maintain and develop it throughout the year.

Devoting thirty rooms in a seventeenth-century stately home to intensive battery-farm rearing of millions of insects that required constant feeding and cleaning was the second massive input of effort and resource. While Zoë herself devoted much time to this, she also had to employ and train workers from the village particularly for the filature process. In addition, the silk farm infrastructure of equipment and machinery required ongoing maintenance.

Lastly, while the by-products from the vast quantities of dead chrysalides were recycled as feed for gamebirds, it was as Zoë explained, a foul-smelling operation.[164] Something of an abbatoir, one imagines, and always would have needed prompt attention.

Chapter Ten

Costing

The involvement in business matters such as import regulations, lobbying the governmental trade officials, the basic economics of running an enterprise, and managing cash flow were never really learned by Zoë: she evidently blundered her way past difficulties, ignoring those who questioned her including Oliver Augustus himself. It is evident from Tom Hart Dyke's account of his grandfather's efforts to save the Lullingstone estate from disaster that the additional burden of Zoë's financial impetuosity in the early and mid-thirties was not the ideal solution at that time

The overhead costs for these investments were not properly considered during the evolution of Zoë's obsession from quirky hobby to industrial-scale enterprise. While Oliver Augustus was on hand to design and craft the spinning and reeling equipment, to make the wooden frames on which the trays of insects spent their short lives, and to build the structures up which the silkworm's instinct drove it for the purpose of spinning a cocoon, there were also the direct costs of purchasing the silkworm eggs and fresh mulberry bush stock each season, and then employing the workforce and paying for the utilities.

Zoë's starting point, that the land and buildings, and her husband Sir Oliver Augustus, were already there and paid for, was actually her limitation. Her activities were envisaged as happening exclusively on a marginal-cost basis, it would seem, when the overall costs should have been identified and spread over a period of years.

In 1937, being unable to answer a question that was often asked of her at exhibitions – about how many silkworms would be needed to make a pair of silk stockings – she wrote to the head of a hosiery firm to ask. The stocking manufacturer's response – which was that the figure could be anything between a hundred and a thousand cocoons – was not helpful to Zoë, so she made up her own estimate reckoning that a safe answer would be about two hundred and fifty silkworms.[165] While this incident gives an idea of the scale of the operation and the breadth of the variables involved in any costing exercises, it also gives us a glimpse into Zoë's tendency to underestimate those costs.

Where did the funding come from?

Zoë herself had brought no wealth into the Hart Dyke family. As we have seen, while the legacy from the Bonds' land in Norfolk and the Mills inheritance had helped to provide servants at home and educational opportunities in her childhood, she was not to inherit what might have been left.

The grand detached house in Leatherhead where Zoë and Oliver Augustus started their family in the early 1920s remained in use by them until well into the 1930s. We also know that the Hart Dyke baronetcy of the nineteen-thirties, while property-rich, was cash-strapped, due to the heavy taxes as detailed elsewhere. Yet Zoë was able to commit expenditure into extensive overseas travel to learn about the silk industry and to find new sources of supply, and funds were available for Oliver Augustus to construct stands at major exhibitions across the country at which Zoë productively spent much time.

Where the money came from is touched on only in one small sentence at the beginning of Zoë's book, where Mrs Crivellari (née Hart Dyke) is mentioned as the person who financed Zoë "with little hope of return."[166] This would appear to be the £20,000 start-up money that is referred to variously in press reports of the time. We will read more detail of this in Chapter Thirteen.

The view from the current Hart Dyke family is that a very small amount of silk was being produced in any one season. It seems infeasible that it could ever have been sufficient to finance Zoë's lifestyle of fact-finding trips abroad and extensive networking in fashionable venues at home. The paying visitors to Lullingstone Castle these days are currently informed that there are some mysteries in this regard that have never been solved, since, as quoted in Chapter Nine, a veil has been drawn over them. The sale of the Leatherhead house and the emptying of the rooms at Lullingstone in order to make way for the silkworms may have yielded income streams, one imagines. However there is no evidence of this.

Economic situation in Britain

There were complex economic pressures in 1930s Britain over which Zoë would have no control and, perhaps, little understanding.

At the time, garment-manufacturing trades were still going strong, but fabric-processing industries such as cotton or wool spinning and weaving were in decline because cheaper raw material, yarns and ready-made fabrics were available from overseas. The silk industry in Britain, apart from a few micro-enterprises, was in a similar position, with spinners and weavers importing raw silk, and selling the resulting material to garment-makers.

In Zoë's case however, she was fully sold on the idea that it was possible to breed and nurture her livestock – the silkworms – as well as manage the associated yarn extraction and spinning. Realistically though, she was happy to do business with the throwers, spinners and garment manufacturers who would complete the finished products. That aspect of the silk production was not her main interest.

Political considerations

The consequent political context that Zoë was able to latch onto was the desire by the British government and the establishment to promote British-made products rather than imports from abroad, particularly from Japan and China. This was the agenda of patriotism and Empire: British workers could, if only given the opportunity, it was posed, produce goods just as well as people in other countries, and Zoë was keen to demonstrate this.

But the economic context was that the silk fabrics and yarn imported in bulk from China and Japan were from sericulture operations based on massive scales of operation. The battleground was therefore not necessarily quality – which Zoë could compete on – but price, which she couldn't.

Although it was her aim to do so, Zoë was never able to offer silk to the British or any other spinners at cheaper prices than those of the major Asian and southern European silk farmers. However her cachet was that she offered British silk processed by British workers.

Zoë's ultimate realisation that the products of the silk farm could be of use to the royal family of the day, not only for their aesthetic qualities but also for their provenance as having been made in Britain, seems to have justified all the efforts, whether "honest" or "dishonest" (see page 51, the confession to the RSA) in her mind.

Zoë eventually seeks business advice

The privations of the Second World War included the banning of luxury item manufacture, but brought with it different – if minor - opportunities for making good use of the Lullingstone estate, as will be explored in the next chapter. It opened new avenues of enquiry for Zoë as she sought financial advice in the shape of Major R. Field Bibb (pictured at Fig. 21), one of the soldiers billeted to Lullingstone during the war. He lent his professional accountancy expertise to the silk farm operations and was subsequently appointed as General Manager and Secretary to the business that was set up in 1946.

Setting up a formal 'limited company' business on the basis of an uncertain performance against heavy investment ratio for several previous years was not the best way to have started. In any case, the pre-war base had been low. A recent academic source[167] states that by 1939 about twenty hectares of mulberries on the plantation at Lullingstone were producing about eleven kilograms of silk per week. In contemporary terms that would seem to constitute about two washing-machine loads.

But indomitably, in 1948 Zoë had even opened an additional enterprise, characterised as the Lullingstone Angora Farm,[168] under the name of North Kent Rabbit Breeders Ltd. with five other directors. Within the year though, this venture had collapsed and the company was struck off the Register.[169] Although reference is made to the experimental start-up of this business, its actual failure is not mentioned in Zoë's autobiography. Unsurprisingly though, the resulting manufacture of the yarn into a bonnet for the future Prince Charles features as a last, nostalgic, reference in her book.[170]

Zoë's funding applications rejected

Following the 1953 coronation, with no other royal occasion immediately on the horizon, Zoë sought business support from the Silk and Rayon Users Association,

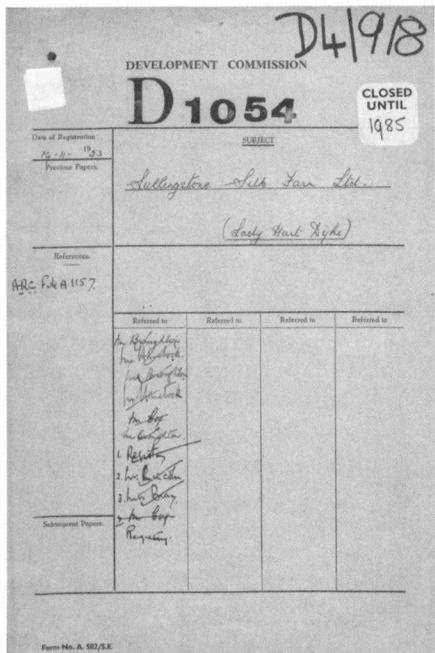

Fig. 18: *Civil Service file on Lullingstone Silk Farm, 1954.*
The National Archives (TNA) Cat Ref D4/918.

whose Chairman was still Sir Ernest Goodale, he who had been her advocate for the 1936 silver medal award at the RSA. As we noted in Chapter Nine, Sir Ernest was also the chairman of Warners Ltd, sole providers of silk to royalty. We will see shortly that Zoë had proposed an arrangement whereby the said Association would assume general and financial control of the Lullingstone Silk Farm.

Meanwhile Zoë had also written, in desperation, personal letters to the Prime Minister and to Buckingham Palace to request financial assistance. The records of her correspondence and the associated minutes detailing how the government eventually said 'No' are in a 1954 one-time confidential Civil Service file of some thirteen documents. (File D1054:[171] see Fig. 18). Zoë's begging letter to Buckingham Palace had been forwarded by the Office of the Privy Purse to the Minister of Agriculture; and her plea to the Prime Minister had been sent on to the Board of Trade. Bewildered civil servants of the Development Commission became the ultimate recipients of both of these requests.

The Secretary of the Development Commission took the view that there were no public funds from which a private business such as the silk farm could expect to receive financial assistance, at the same time offered advice about ways of organising the enterprise. A letter to this effect was sent to Zoë on 19 November 1953.

According to a minute dated 26 January 1954, Zoë had written back to the Development Commission to say, quite firmly, that cash, not advice, was what she needed. There then followed an attempt by the civil servants to get a review of the Development Commission Secretary's decision. But even an appeal to the Treasury that had been made because of:

> "... the eminence of the people with whom Lady Hart Dyke had corresponded, and the use which had been made of the silk..."[172]

gave rise to the same negative result. The Treasury gave a firm 'No' when asked directly if the reasons of national prestige could be cited to rescue the silk farm.

Chapter Ten

The civil servants were at pains to ascribe due reasons for this outcome. A case was made that the economic prospect of the company was poor because of the competition of imported silk and new fibres on the market. Quoting an obscure governmental report[173] from 1938 that public investment would be required over a long period in order to set up a natural silk industry, the civil servants advised the Minister that in any case such an endeavour would not be of vital national importance.

Details were recorded that Zoë had declared a deficit of £2,500 and her own personal resources totally exhausted. Her venture in valve assembly at Lullingstone was short-lived and had yielded no financial gain. The main income of the silk farm was from the provision of teas and sale of souvenirs to visitors.

The fact that Zoë had directed her letters to:

> " ... various people connected with the Court or eminent in public life..."[174]

did no favours to her case, as far as the civil servants were concerned. And judging from this remark by a senior officer of the Development Commission about Lullingstone's yield, Zoë's plight was likely to have been the source of some mirth:

> "I gathered also that silk for the last two Coronations has been produced though, ironically, Lady Hart Dyke attributes the present financial difficulties of the farm largely to the Coronation in 1953 because the number of visitors to the farm was much diminished by reason of counter-attractions in London."[175]

Notwithstanding all this, the civil servants had an unrivalled card to play. Sir Ernest Goodale, after receiving Zoë's request for support, had sent a Mr Carthy, the Secretary of the Silk and Rayon Users Association, to conduct an examination of the Lullingstone Silk Farm company's affairs. Certain information from this examination, namely that £5,000 was needed immediately with a further £1,000 for the following three years to "put the enterprise on its feet" had somehow been "conveyed in strict confidence" to the Board of Trade.

The confidentiality was such that not even Zoë had been told. Note 3 in Document 1 of File D1054 continues:

> "The Association had turned her down but so far as we know, the outcome of this investigation was not communicated to Lady Hart Dyke, and she is probably unaware of it. It follows that if it became known to her that use had been made of these findings in considering her case she might take exception both to the use of the information and to the conclusions reached, on which she has had no opportunity of commenting."

Furthermore Zoë's proposal that the farm could become:

> " ... a demonstration and propaganda centre with the Association controlling the propaganda and assuming the control of general and financial policy in return for financial assistance..."

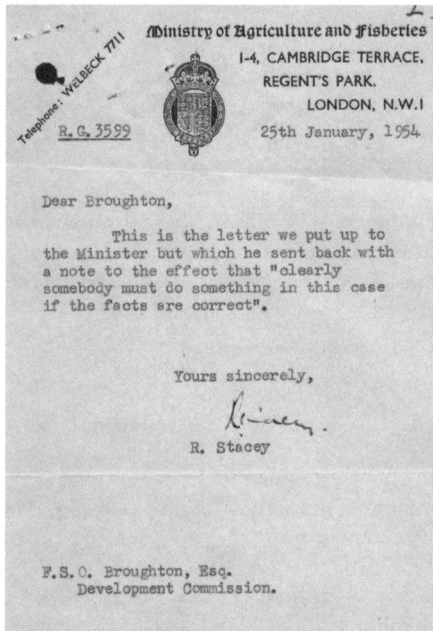

Fig. 19: How Zoë's funding appeal was considered, 1954.
The National Archives (TNA) Cat Ref D4/918.

was mentioned in the (unseen) covering memorandum from Mr Carthy to the Silk and Rayon Users Association Executive Committee. Sir Ernest Goodale's report was ordered to be separated from Mr Carthy's memorandum before being sent to the Board of Trade on 1 February 1954.

The explanatory Document 3 of File D1054[176] formed the final minute to be placed on the records of the Ministry of Agriculture.

It appears that Zoë had been betrayed by the Silk and Rayon Users.

Having heard of the bizarre developments that had followed the initial rejection of Zoë's request for funding, the Chairman of the Development Commission had felt obliged to intervene firmly, saying that the Commission would not associate itself with any application for funding from the Lullingstone Silk Farm and that the Ministry of Agriculture and Fisheries and the Board of Trade should be so informed.

The civil servants had received the opinion of the Minister on 25 January 1954 (see Fig. 19)[177] that something needed to be done. One could be forgiven for thinking that these events were taken from an episode of BBC TV's satirical *Yes Minister*.[178]

Evidently nothing was done, other than a rejection letter to Zoë, and the file was held back from public availability until 1985, ten years after her death.

The Lullingstone Silk Farm at Lullingstone was clearly unable to meet its commitments, and within two years had transferred to the heart of the silk weaving industry at Ayot St Lawrence, Hertfordshire.

Grandson Tom had an apt summary for her:

> "Zoë was a marvel all right. But all dreams have their price and, as a businesswoman, my dynamic grandma was nothing if not a walking financial disaster area."[179]

Chapter Eleven: Lullingstone in the 1940s

The war years had meant the cessation of silk production for garments, and its direct use to support the war effort was discontinued fairly early on. Resuming in 1946 was a brave attempt. Clothing rations continued well into the 1950s and few people could have afforded even silk squares, stockings or ties, let alone fashionable outfits made from this luxury yarn.

With silk being off the approved purchase in people's ration books, Zoë assured her former school journal that she was:

> "... housing three and a half million warworkers at Lullingstone Castle. These are silkworms, and they are busy producing silk for use in parachutes."[180]

However the unsuitability of the Lullingstone silk and the low output curtailed the activity. Zoë blamed the government for the impact of trade restrictions in 1934, (as she had complained to the RSA earlier) on her imported supplies.[181]

Zoë and the armed forces

During the later years of the war Zoë's connections with overseas silk production broadened, and she advised monks in Ireland, and growers in Cyprus, Canada and The Congo; the former two benefiting from a personal visit. Judging from her jolly account of flying by an unreliable Dakota to Cyprus from Herne airport in Kent via Marseilles and Cairo,[182] Zoë comes across as being an indefatigable British colonial traveller.

But initially during the war, Lulllingstone estate had been commandeered as a "battle school". Zoë calmly claims in her book that she was taught how to kill or disable a man with the aid of a short stick.[183] I get the impression that, had she needed to, Zoë would not have hesitated to make use of this skill.

The Royal Air Force (RAF) was the last of the armed forces to be billeted at Lullingstone in the war, with the estate at that time being turned into a decoy airfield for the protection of the nearby Biggin Hill operational air base.

This wartime period and the unprecedented events during them have elicited in Zoë's entertaining book some of her best anecdotal throwaways and quotations. My front-runner for her most iconic quotation is the following:

> "In the middle of the silkworm season the R. A .M. C.[184] left and rumours were flying that (1) French Canadians, (2) The Black Watch, (3) an unnamed Indian regiment – were to replace them, so I brushed up my French, read all about haggis in an encyclopaedia, ate curry at an Indian restaurant and awaited events."

In the event it was the United States Army that turned up, about whom Zoë's next remark has to be one of the most shameless:

> "Both white and coloured, my Americans were delightful guests. I must confess I was rather shaken to find armfuls of flowers and cigarettes and marvellous tinned food piled up on my desk every other day or so, but when I remonstrated with the donors, they were genuinely hurt, so I stifled my conscience, and ruined my figure, and enjoyed a blissful four months of being thoroughly spoilt."

The divorce

During the Second World War Oliver Augustus' engineering skills were put to use full-time in the running of technical production facilities for the war effort elsewhere in England, leaving Lullingstone very much to Zoë. This was not without repercussions, and their marriage would not be the only one about to falter under separation imposed by war.

Zoë's characteristic avoidance of the personal, combined with her very English sense of understatement, caused her to record the rift between Oliver Augustus and herself solely as being of consequence to the business in 1946:

> "Oliver had his hands full, and he asked us whether we would mind if he resigned from the Board and started his own little engineering works. He was anxious to make not only reeling machinery but other types of machinery as well, and felt he simply hadn't time to do everything thoroughly, so very sadly we agreed to his proposal."[185]

In fact the marriage had ended two years prior to that. In a press article[186] headed 'Decree Against Baronet, Blamed Nerves for Indifference', news had broken that Zoë had been granted a divorce from Oliver Augustus on grounds of the adultery of her husband:

> "The case for Lady Hart-Dyke was that after 1930 there was a change in her husband's manner, and he had no interest in her as a wife. She taxed him with her indifference, and he said it was due to nerves.[187] In 1943 he began to stay away from home, and last August she received a letter enclosing an hotel bill."

The citing of the 1930 date seems particularly sad, since the couple had spent a holiday in Las Palmas during that year from 6 March to 3 April, sailing from the Port of London.[188] Though this might have been planned as a carefree break for the couple since the children did not accompany them, it took place during what turned out to be Oliver Augustus' last year before inheriting the Lullingstone estate and all its responsibilities.

The fact that her marriage to Oliver Augustus had ended meant that Zoë was no longer entitled to be styled 'Lady Zoë Hart Dyke' and the link to the baronetcy was severed.

Chapter Eleven

But there was no apparent diminution of the royal patronage of the silk garments and fabrics, and Zoë continued to run the farm activities, living on the Lullingstone estate during this time, albeit in one of the cottages.

The royal wedding of 1947, in which Princess Elizabeth's dress was made from Lullingstone silk, was attended on behalf of the farm by the Company Secretary Major R. Field Bibb and Miss Standen, the Forewoman. To Zoë's credit, any disappointment at missing the royal occasion was firmly swallowed and did not come through in the writing.

Late in 1945 Oliver Augustus married Mildred T. Berens at Chelsea. In 1947, under his own business name, he exhibited his power reelers and hand reelers for silk at an exhibition at Earls Court.[189] The Kensington and Chelsea electoral registers for Chelsea record a residence for 'Dyke, Oliver (Sir)' at 278 Chelsea Cloisters from 1949 to 1952. In 1952 Sir Oliver and Mildred moved back to the Bothy Cottage at Lullingstone before taking up residence at the castle in 1956.[190]

Zoë after the divorce

It must have been a delicate situation during those ten post-war years. The silk farm was in operation but Zoë was no longer the 'Lady' of the estate on which it existed. Although she was working without the business backing of Oliver Augustus, she had taken the precaution of including their son Derek (then Flight Sergeant D. W. Hart Dyke RAF and heir to the baronetcy), on the Board.[191]

She spent time writing two accounts of the actual silk farm: short booklets published in 1945 and 1947 (See *Select Bibliography and References 4*). A later one was to come in 1955 (*Select Bibliography and References 1*). Her autobiography was published in 1949, and I have wondered how she ever had the time to write it. I was not surprised to read that she had help from Major R Field Bibb in the proof-reading and editing of her text.

Zoë never remarried, but as we will see in the next chapter, her relationship with Major R Field Bibb, who remained married, was to blossom and endure until his death just a few years before her own.

Lullingstone silk head-squares, Jacqmar and Arnold Lever

Although Zoe's exuberant account in her autobiography of the 1948 "Silver Jubilee of our loved King and Queen"[192] should have more accurately referenced merely the *Daily Mail*'s Silver Jubilee of the Ideal Home exhibition[193] at Olympia, it had nevertheless provided her with an opportunity for royal networking, which is perhaps what caused her confusion about the occasion's purpose.

Zoë's stand there offered the epitome of quality and pedigree of the war-time and post-war fashion for silk head-squares. She writes about two examples of head-squares made from Lullingstone silk, and it is here that we become aware of her business connection with Arnold Lever, the still-celebrated designer of cult textile company Jacqmar.[194]

> "The first [head-square] was designed by that clever artist, Arnold Lever, and was produced for Jacqmar. The design showed the various stages of silk production. Inside a large mulberry leaf were the intermingled parts of our reeling machinery, complete with cocoons, scales, a 'book' of silk, and other things – and crawling up the thick stem of the leaf was a fat silkworm wearing a pink crown on his head like a beret."[195]

Zoë notes with joy that this was the silk scarf on the stand that was chosen by Princess Elizabeth as a gift from Lullingstone Silk Farm. My research has revealed four examples of that design which are identical to Zoë's description, all attributed to Arnold Lever with a signature and 'Lullingstone Silk Farm' inscribed on the imagery. This confirms that more than one scarf was printed, as is normal, and it is apparent from the images I have seen that each differed slightly in colour.

One of the three scarves is at the Boston Museum of Fine Arts, with a stated provenance of having been purchased in London. Although it is not displayed visually on the website, it is described in detail with mention of a grey background. A second one with a beige colour to the mulberry leaf surface is owned by designer Lulu Guinness.[196] A third one on a pink background[197] was sold by a London auctioneer[198] in 2008.

The image on the inside front cover shows the original head-square retained in the Arnold Lever Archive. The design of these four silk squares closely resembles the sketch, initialled by Arnold Lever and attributed to him, on the dust-jacket of Zoë's autobiography, in which a mulberry leaf is about to be eaten by an infeasible tiara-wearing silkworm (See *Selected Bibliography and References 1*).

The Duchess of Kent was reported by Zoë to have received the second, more traditional, head-square example at the *Daily Mail* exhibition stand. It was a Paisley design printed by Liberty.

Chapter Eleven

Zoë's health

A particular challenge for Zoë was some kind of incident that placed her in hospital for some time (unspecified). She didn't think it worth mentioning in the autobiography, but she did report the circumstance to *Paulina*, where a note appeared in March 1947.

> "ZOE BOND, 1905 – 13 (Lady Hart Dyke) wrote to Muriel Walmsley in December from hospital where she was a patient with a broken patella. Orders were streaming in to her silk-worm farm, but she would be delighted to show a party of Paulinas round it before she is overwhelmed with business."

Four years later in 1951 we find a further spell of confinement had necessitated a second visit from John Nolan of the *National Geographic* magazine (see *Selected Bibliography and References* 2) owing to his first visit having taken place:

> "… while I was tucked away out of mischief, on a plaster bed, with a cracked spine."[199]

She does seem to have suffered the most awful bad luck.

Chapter Twelve: Hertfordshire and beyond

Fig. 20: Zoë Lady Hart Dyke leaves Lullingstone Castle, 1956.
Photo credit: TopFoto.

Zoë's move in 1956 from Lullingstone to Hertfordshire involved the transfer of the silk farm itself, as well as her own residence. The precise circumstances of Zoë's departure, which came two years after the unsuccessful application for government funding, are not fully known, although the new location for the silk farm at Ayot St Lawrence makes business sense given the preponderance of silk weavers and spinners[200] at the time in that part of Hertfordshire. I make the assumption that Major Field Bibb had some influence on the new location.

The photograph shown at Fig. 20 indicates that Zoë, as ever, used an opportunity to make a definitive statement about this significant change in her life. Sporting a crash helmet and dressed in a duffel coat, sheepskin gauntlets and high-heeled shoes, Zoë is seen posing in front of the Lullingstone Castle Gatehouse riding a very trendy scooter, replete with side-car.

Zoë's new location turned out to be just opposite George Bernard Shaw's former residence 'Shaw Corner'.[201] The celebrated writer and philosopher had died there in 1950 and the house that he had lived in for forty years was soon opened to the inquisitive public.[202] This provided her with ready-made cohorts of visitors and Zoë quickly made the most of the happy co-location by writing in the publicity:

> "Five minutes' walk from the home of the late Bernard Shaw - why not visit both?"[203]

Ayot House was given a grand opening on 1 April 1957 when Zoë hired film star Jill Adams to perform the opening ceremony.[204]

Moving on a decade later a report in *Paulina* (see Appendix 4 extract 2) reveals that a party of former pupils made a visit to Zoë's silk farm at Ayot St Lawrence on 8 June 1968. They had been made very welcome and were amazed at Zoë's evident achievements. Part of this success is explained by the continued support from Major Field Bibb.

Major R. Field Bibb 1902 – 1971

We know that in 1946 the Major had been appointed to a financial role in the newly-established silk farm enterprise Lullingstone Silk Farm Ltd.. On investigation of public records, I found out that he remained involved with the company until his death on 27 April 1971 at Hitchin, Hertfordshire aged 69.

Appearing in Zoë's autobiography as second on the list of people to thank was indeed the Major R. Field Bibb. However while he rose from a Captain to being a Major (of the Wessex Territorials[205]) during the period covered in her book, and although he is only ever addressed by his military title throughout, her thanks to him on the initial pages of the book are discreetly limited to:

> " … the many hours he has spent bringing order out of chaos by marshalling a spate of words into orderly chapters, and for correcting both statistics and spelling."[206]

Zoë later introduces him in more detail to her readers as one of the Army officers stationed at Lullingstone in the Second World War, explaining, as we have noted, that he helped her with the financial side of the business since he was an accountant by profession. She intimates:

> "Just before he left for overseas he told me that he would really like to join me at the Farm after the war, and take up the work seriously."[207]

We can see from the image at Fig. 21, where Major Field Bibb leads Zoë and the workers in the procession at the 1948 Harvest Festival of the World at Canterbury Cathedral that he did return after the war. Zoë and five of her women workers are dressed in turban and smock-overalls and Zoë carries a tray of silk-moth cocoons. Major R. Field Bibb, captioned as 'manager', strides ahead of Zoë carrying Lullingstone Silk Farm's own banner. The marchers behind them could possibly be the "two buxom Land Girls"[208] that she employed in her market garden in wartime. This image was originally published in a main feature about Zoë in *National Geographic* magazine.[209]

The occasion is laden with symbolism, given what we know about Zoë's passion, and could almost have masqueraded as a nuptial event had it not been for the fact that the Major ten years previously had married one Vera Doris Kay Mead, a "spinster" aged

33, at the parish church of Weston-Super-Mare. His profession was given on their 1938 certificate as 'accountant'.[210] A daughter, Jacqueline Susan Field Bibb, was born to the couple at the same town in 1941.[211] This was around the time that he was stationed at Lullingstone, from where, as we have seen, he was then posted abroad.

Fig. 21: Harvest Festival of the World, *Canterbury Cathedral, 19 June 1948. Zoë (with tray) follows Major Field Bibb (with banner). Photo credit: TopFoto.*

Given that his association with Zoë was to be lifelong, I tried to establish something about the Major's background. Ronald Field Bibb had been born in 1902 at Kings Norton, Worcestershire, the son of a brass founders' traveller Samuel Isaiah Bibb and Hilda Maud Bibb (née Field).[212] Before acquiring the accounting skills that made him so useful to Zoë, Ronald Field Bibb (when aged 17) had arrived at Boston MA on the *Sosua* on 5 June 1919,[213] and landed at New York in March 1920 on the SS *Verentia* the latter occasion as a paid-off seaman having been discharged at Avonmouth on 7 February 1920.[214]

He was thus no stranger to overseas travel, something also likely to have been useful to Zoë, whose constant need for imports of silkworm eggs and mulberry plants had been so drastically interrupted by the war. Having first been stationed at Lullingstone in 1941, Major Field Bibb went on to make useful connections in Cyprus where he persuaded the Director of Agriculture to send fresh mulberry seed and silkworm stock to Zoë.[215]

At his end it was Zoë who was the informant of death in 1971, giving his occupation and usual address as "Company Director (Silk Farm) at Ayot House, Ayot St Lawrence", and she was named on the certificate as the person responsible for his burial.[216]

Notwithstanding Ronald Field Bibb's evident close relationship with Zoë, Vera Doris Kay Bibb outlived her husband, becoming his widow for ten years until she remarried, aged 76, in 1981. How long her partnership with second husband Joseph Horace Ellis, a widower aged 78, had existed prior to their 1981 marriage is not known, but she was to live only three months more after marrying him. Her own daughter, Jacqueline Susan Field Bibb was the informant of her death.[217]

Lullingstone silk 1950s – 1980s

Subsequent to the 1953 coronation two royal weddings (Princess Margaret's in 1960 and Princess Anne's in 1973) were to take place and there was also the Investiture of the Prince of Wales at Caernarvon in 1969. All of these entailed the use of Lullingstone silk. The latter was specifically credited by Sir Ernest Goodale of Warners with Zoë's silk as having been used;[218] the former occasions' involvement is referred to more obliquely on the Lullingstone Silk Farm brochure 1970 (see *Selected Bibliography and References 5*).

The later years in Hertfordshire were characterised by Zoe's failing health and solitude following the death of Major Field Bibb. Subsequent to Zoë's own death in 1975 the whole enterprise was sold, interestingly, to lepidopterist Robert Goodden, as noted in Chapter Three. The mulberry bushes, silkworm stocks and equipment were moved, as a going concern, to Compton House near Sherborne in Dorset, where Goodden incorporated the silk-moths with his butterfly farm thereby setting up the Worldlife and Lullingstone Farm.[219] It was from here that the silk for Lady Diana Spencer's 1981 wedding dress was spun.[220]

The young designers of Lady Diana Spencer's dress, which was described at the time as a 'meringue' dress with 'leg o'mutton' sleeves, had abandoned the mid-century traditional design of Norman Hartnell. However the desire to use British-made silk was still as politically desirable in the 1980s as it had been in the 1930s, hence David and Elizabeth Emmanuel decided to incorporate Lullingstone silk into their fashion statement creation.

But not everyone was enamoured with the quality of this post-Zoë Lullingstone silk.

A recent assessment is:

> "The Emmanuels' biggest mistake was to use silk from Lullingstone, the only silk farm in the UK. They should have used French silk rather than the English stuff which crumpled like toilet paper. But they got away with it."[221]

This was the very last royal order for Lullingstone silk. Goodden's operations closed in 2004 and the fate and whereabouts of any descendant *bombycidae* are not known.

A rather sad end to Zoë's efforts.

Chapter Thirteen: Zoë's sponsors and influences

At any period in the twentieth century it would have demanded a particularly adventurous woman to reach a pinnacle of achievement in a highly competitive textile process manufacturing industry. Zoë had a flying start. Her financially-comfortable middle-class roots, her natural curiosity, her determination and interest in practical skills would all have been boosted by the enlightened educational experiences and by having fended for herself as a young adult through the post-First World War years. But she also undoubtedly had that extra helping of eccentricity and single-mindedness that led her to intervene with direct action whenever a problem needed to be solved and to discard obstacles.

The period from the procreation of her family to Zoë's nationally-important achievement in sericulture gives rise to some fascinating social detail of the time since she also benefited from the support of key backers, some of whom were pioneering and unusual women of the time.

Mrs Crivellari 1873 – 1964

Of primary importance to Zoë's success was an earlier seeker of feminine emancipation. Coming from the Hart Dyke family itself, this ally was Mrs Crivellari, whose role we first noted in Chapter Ten. At the beginning of her autobiography Zoë had expressed thanks to those who helped or encouraged her in the silk farm venture. Mrs Crivellari was first on this list, and her inclusion is credited by Zoë as being due to:

> " … her faith in my venture since its inception, and for the ungrudging way she financed me with little hope of return."[222]

Mrs Crivellari (pictured in Fig. 22) was the eldest of Sir William and Lady Emily Caroline Hart Dyke's offspring, having been born in 1873. She was thus Zoë's sister-in-law, although she was old enough to have been her mother. (See Appendix 2A for the Hart Dyke ancestry diagram). Married twice and with just one son, Lina Mary Crivellari was active in politics and voluntary work, serving on the Huntingdonshire County Council and various hospital and school boards. Having switched from Conservative to Liberal Party membership she was later awarded an OBE in 1918 for voluntary service[223] and in 1924 she was elected to the Council of the Women's National Liberal Federation.[224]

In 1902 she married Alexander Scott Gatty, who was an actor from a titled family.[226] They divorced in 1926, by which time their only son Edward was aged twenty-three. In 1931 Edward pre-deceased his mother, and in that same year she married Captain Antonio Crivellari. Not long afterwards her father and mother, Sir William and Lady Emily Hart Dyke, also both died. As noted elsewhere, the backdrop to these events was her brother Oliver Augustus' actions in downsizing the Lullingstone estate in order to meet the double death duties of their parents. Lina Mary and Captain Crivellari married just two months after these deaths.

Solemnised at the Register Office of St Marylebone on 7 September 1931[227] the marriage of 58 years old Lina Mary, four years a divorcee,[228] with 63 years old Antonio Crivellari, a widower and retired captain of the Merchant Marine living on independent means, took place. 'Oliver H. Dyke' (Oliver Augustus) was the first-listed witness at the wedding; a person cited as 'Florence Duncombe' was the second. The full name and title of the latter was Lady Anne Florence Adelaide Duncombe (née Montagu). A widow with no offspring,[229] she was actually the sister of the recently deceased Lady Emily Caroline Hart Dyke (née Montagu), whom she was to outlive by another nine years. In other words, she was an aunt of Lina Mary.

Captain Crivellari never appeared on any voters' list, although Lina Mary did, listed as living in the Marylebone Ward of Westminster.[230] This would indicate that the captain did not own the property or, on the other hand perhaps did not have British citizenship. Nevertheless on his eventual death in 1954 at a Harley Street clinic[231] Antonio Crivellari left a significant amount: £11,107, and Lina Mary continued to live in their home until shortly before her own demise in 1964, leaving £34,818.[232]

The source(s) of Lina Mary's funds invested in the silk farm enterprise are thus likely to be family wealth, but from precisely which family, whether Hart Dyke or Crivellari, is not recorded. It could be that Lina Mary's second marriage provided a financial boost to the Hart Dyke estate, some part of which may have become the quoted £20,000[233] start-up sum for the silk farm. However it is also probable that the marriage may have helped to separate out some funds from the Hart Dyke previous generation thus reducing the death duty burden.

Lina Mary's strong participation in Victorian and Edwardian public life is interesting in comparison with the lifestyle of her mother, Lady Emily Caroline Hart Dyke who, as mentioned earlier, was the extraordinary drummer and cane chair-repairer featured in the family group photograph at Fig. 15.

Financially, Zoë's quest was never going to succeed on its own, so the two women - Lina Mary and Zoë - might seem well - matched on a number of counts. The eccentric and ambitious Zoë might have been a welcome protégée for the bereaved and wealthy Lina Mary Crivellari, given the evident unconventional streak in the Hart Dyke maternal background.

Fig: 22 Lina Mary Scott Gatty (née Hart Dyke) 1918, later to become Lina Mary Crivellari.[225]
Image by permission of Imperial War Museum

Chapter Thirteen

Miss Joan Ryder 1905 – 1985

Zoë's peers in business included contacts made at the many commercial fairs and exhibitions to which the Lullingstone Silk Farm stand was taken. Let's move to 1939, and picture Zoë in Brighton at the *Home Life Exhibition* at the Dome and Corn Exchange organised by the Grocers' Association. Zoë herself had been invited to open this exhibition, an invitation to which she succumbed – guiltily – since it meant deferring work on the mulberry plantation.[234]

It was at the Exhibitors' Club there that she spied a person who was to become a firm lifelong friend: Miss Joan Ryder, daughter of Samuel Ryder of Ryder Cup[236] fame. Zoë writes:

> "She had a cocktail in one hand and a cigarette in the other, and after I was similarly equipped, we began to talk ....".[237]

Zoë's description of this first meeting with Joan Ryder evokes a particular vision of 1930s' society that her own adventurousness, and social status, had enabled her to join and inhabit.

Fig. 23: Joan Ryder, cigarette and umbrella in hand, early 1930s. [235] *Courtesy of Tom Ryder.*

Joan Ryder had been exhibiting pot-pourri at Brighton when Zoë encountered her. Joan herself had become involved in business by taking over her family's highly successful garden seed packet enterprise 'Heath & Heather'[238] on her father's death. Zoë's close association with Joan was to result notably in the creation of a herb garden at Lullingstone through Joan's recommending[239] the involvement of Miss Sinclair Rohde as designer[240] but apparently doing much of the work herself.[241]

Joan's key role in Zoë's life arguably was as chairman of Lullingstone Farm Ltd from 1946.[242] Zoë does not attribute any specific business expertise to Joan's involvement, but Joan, with her own successful business experience in horticultural retail, may well have been the one who encouraged Zoë to diversify by selling ranges of merchandise at Ayot St Lawrence. This merchandise seems to have been significant and the impression I gained from seeing the extent of visitor material produced during the silk farm's existence at Ayot St Lawrence is that more money was likely to have been accrued from entrance fees and peripherals. However exporting silk cocoons seems to have been the mainstay (see Chapter Fourteen).

As we have seen Zoë had written and published booklets on sericulture and the history of Lullingstone Silk Farm, and she created children's literature around a silkworm character named Sebastian. She knew from her own experience that it was very much a childhood hobby. She also put on sale at Ayot St Lawrence real cocoons, silkworm eggs, skeins of silk, students' silk-making kits, silk scarves, ties and handkerchiefs. See the 1969 Price List in *Selected Bibliography and References 5*.

Mary Benedetta 1909 – [243]

In 1937 Zoë had been interviewed by the renowned writer and film-maker Mary Benedetta at Alexandra Palace for BBC TV. In Zoë's words, Mary was:

> "... a frail young girl with masses of golden curls all over her head ... it seemed impossible that this vision had written books, travelled all over the world, produced films".[244]

At the point of meeting Zoë, Mary had just finished writing, in association with Bauhaus photographer Moholy-Nagy, an explosive account of London's street life.[245] This ground-breaking volume features junk merchants, antique dealers, costermongers, hucksters, barrowmen and more. All this seemed to have fascinated Zoë, for whom it would have been a hitherto undiscovered world.

Mary later wrote film-scripts and scenarios for the war effort and post-war government information, including *General Election,* 1949, featuring John Profumo as an MP. Her connection with film was much appreciated by Zoë, who writes glowingly of Mary's visit to the Lullingstone Silk Farm stand at the 1948 *Ideal Home Exhibition* (as mentioned in Chapter Eleven) bringing along a famous film star of the day Edana Romney.[246] Zoë was all for name-dropping.

In Mary, Zoë seems to have found a cross-over character, equally at home in the unconventional and creative culture as well as the burgeoning current affairs circles. During the war, still finding the time to travel to London, Zoë accepted an invitation from Mary Benedetta to a cocktail party.

Mrs Henderson 1863 – 1944

At the cocktail party, Zoë met Mrs Laura Henderson, a woman somewhat senior to herself, having been born in 1863. Laura Henderson was to offer the inquisitive Zoë some glimpses into even more salacious aspects of London society and the entertainment world than had their mutual friend Mary Benedetta.

She has been summarised as:

> " ... an eccentric British socialite ... [who] rose to prominence in the 1930s when, as a wealthy and eccentric widow, she founded the Windmill Theatre".[248]

Chapter Thirteen

Fig. 24: Mrs Laura Henderson[247] c. 1940, whose contribution to the entertainment world has been immortalised in the 2005 film Mrs Henderson Presents. Courtesy of David Rose.

This theatre in London's West End had become famous for lawfully staging female nudity in live shows, the technicalities of which Mrs Henderson was routinely challenged on by the censor's officials. An article in *The Independent* of 2007 cited that:

> " ... letters from the Lord Chamberlain's office say she [Laura Henderson] had been able to twist people in the office around her little finger."[249]

Zoë writes that she often accompanied Mrs Henderson to the shows at the Windmill and remarks:

> "To see her sitting bolt upright in her box – very *grand dame* – watching her 'children' perform the gayest and most frivolous turns imaginable was indeed an education." [250]

But these enlightening experiences apart, there perhaps wasn't too much for her to learn from Mrs Henderson's apparently equally persuasive skills of getting people to do things.

Notably though, Zoë's additional attraction to Laura was the latter's possession of a mulberry tree, the leaves of which supplemented the inadequacy of supplies from the Lullingstone plantation.

Unravelling the Yarn

Fig. 25: Fashion Theatre, Women of Empire Pavilion, Empire Exhibition Glasgow 1938²⁵². SC760084 © Courtesy of HES.

Miss Margaret Brodie 1907 – 1997, and Lady Elgin c.1900 – 1989

Somewhat earlier, Zoë had been asked to create a silk farm exhibit at the incredible Glasgow 1938 *Empire Exhibition*, in a pavilion dedicated to women's achievements that had been designed by architect Miss Margaret Brodie. Born about three years later than Zoë, Margaret Brodie of Largs, Ayrshire, was to become celebrated as an eminent architect for whom this pavilion, in Glasgow's Bellahouston Park,[251] and the on-site supervision of more than a hundred other exhibition constructions, would be her own pinnacle of achievement. This was an extraordinary feat in the male-dominated world of architecture.

Margaret Brodie's Women of the Empire Pavilion alone housed three exhibition halls, a Fashion Theatre (see Fig. 25) and tearooms – all run entirely by women under a committee headed by the Countess of Elgin[253] and Mrs Walter Elliot who was described as the wife of the Secretary of State for Scotland. The Fashion Theatre held shows four times per day, displaying British designs and fabrics. There is no specific mention of Lullingstone silk garments being modelled but Zoë personally kept topped up the Lullingstone stand every ten days for six months. She enthused about the spectacle of all manner of women's craft and creations in the pavilion and reported that her stand proved lucrative in terms of silk scarf sales.[254]

Chapter Thirteen

The scheduled date of the royal opening of the *Empire Exhibition* was going to pose a silk-worm breeding schedule problem for Zoë, so in an effort to show live silk-worms in the unseasonal May, she went on an advance trip to Glasgow, staying with Lady Elgin for a weekend during which she scoured the city for mulberry trees. Hoping to find a mulberry owner who would force[255] some branches for her, Zoë was in the end disappointed to find only one specimen of the tree. It was in the grounds of the magnificent Kelvingrove, but was not even in bud. So, disappointingly, the silkworms used on the Lullingstone stand in the pavilion had to be the artificial ones previously used for the televised appearances with Mary Benedetta.

Lady Katharine Elgin was operating in a stratum of society rather beyond the one which Zoë had reached, and her public work, including that of the *Empire Exhibition*, was recognised during her lifetime by the award of the DBE.

Architect Margaret Brodie on the other hand was very much a hands-on professional career woman. A critic wrote of Margaret Brodie later:

> "In her dress, femme fatale was juxtaposed with tweedy county woman. At the opening of the Empire Exhibition on 3 May 1938, newspapers reported her stunning appearance in the most glamorous ensemble. This feminine figure, ready to have a cigarette with Queen Mary, could be quickly replaced by an old pair of cords and a shirt and tie ready to deal with a troublesome contractor."[256]

It's not impossible that such a description might also have been made about Zoë. Perhaps the two women shared some characteristics and outlooks on life. They both, reportedly, cut tall and assertive figures, and together present a fascinatingly speculative image of their business alliance.

However, an obituary,[257] while recording that Miss Brodie's students at the Royal College Glasgow (where she was the only woman on the staff) regarded her as hardworking and outlandish, also notes that her eccentricity and bluffness were but a mask and that:

> "Miss Brodie was in fact a very shy and deeply sensitive woman, who had succeeded in a male-dominated occupation. Despite this she hated feminism: 'Never be a feminist, that's important', she would advise her young female friends."

This certainly contrasts with Zoë's unremittingly outgoing nature.

Yet the quotation about feminism – which I interpret from within the context of the era – may also have been something in which both Margaret and Zoë would have found some common ground. Later we will see that Zoë indeed rejects any apologetic excuses for her own involvement as a woman in business.

Brodie, Elgin, Hart Dyke and feminism of the era

Miss Brodie, the Countess of Elgin and Zoë Lady Hart Dyke had all made significant achievements in male-dominated environments, each in a contrasting way.

Miss Margaret Brodie's lone work as a woman in the creative but disciplined profession of architecture saw her idiosyncrasies being tolerated but not necessarily celebrated by those around her. This contrasts with the milieu of Zoë's more ostentatious companions from the London fashionable set in which gender discrimination may have constituted a different kind of issue, with accompanying flamboyance or eccentricity something to be expected. By contrast, the loftily-titled Katherine Elgin combined an adherence to a gender-stereotypical role with her stoical public work rooted in the expectations of her social class.

The imperial context would have imposed its own limitations on the portrayal of the statuses of women from the various parts of the British Empire, and Zoë's role, connected as it was with fashion, would not have broadened that. However all three of these leading women shared the expectation that not only were there worthwhile reflections to be made of the life and contribution of women, but that these should be organised and exhibited by women too.

Historically overall, the Glasgow 1938 *Empire Exhibition* tragically was eclipsed by its timing immediately prior to the Second World War. As far as I know, Zoë's part in the Women of Empire Pavilion has not yet been recorded outside this account and her autobiography.

Chapter Fourteen:
Dr & Mrs Bond and their Leyton-born offspring
Zoë's last known links with her birth family

Let us step back to glimpse into the lives of Zoë's parents, Barnabas Mayston Bond and Eliza Josephine Bond (née Luxon). To recap, Zoë, in her early twenties, and her elder sister Elsie Margaret left the Hammersmith family home later than their other siblings. Walter Tremayne had first left home for Vancouver, Canada, but at the outbreak of the First World War he returned and, as noted earlier, went into the army, joining up with the Honourable Artillery Company in 1915.[258] Sylvia Christine, as we have seen, was married in 1918.

The assertion by Zoë, as already noted, that in 1919 Dr Bond had sold his practice and premises in order to move to France with Eliza Josephine for the benefit of her health, is the last we hear of them. Indeed there is nothing to suggest that Zoë ever met them again.

Zoë's marriage into the Hart Dykes and the subsequent raising of a family with three children is not depicted in her book as having any significance in Barnabas and Eliza's lives. There are no words of her parents being pleased, satisfied or impressed with her, no mention of the children's Bond grandparents being involved in family life. This underlines what her grandson Tom had written about her maternal track record, as we saw in Chapter Nine.

Moreover, Zoë's own maternal grandmother, the widow Eliza Tremain Luxon from Cornwall who may have lived with the Bonds from the Leyton days onwards, is not included in Zoë's written memories. That said, her death aged 76 on 21 February 1913 at Hammersmith would have coincided with Zoë's time at the Collège des Jeunes Filles in France and hence may have reduced any impact on her. Eliza Luxon left a modest "£254.12s.6d.[259] effects to Eliza Josephine Bond [her daughter] wife of Barnabas Mayston Bond" according to the official records.[260]

The question arises as to what caused an irreconcilable rift in the Bond family. Perhaps it was Zoë's continued obsession with silkworms beyond childhood as suggested in Chapter Three, perhaps it was her lack of coming up to Barnabas's expectations in education and employment, or perhaps it was her bohemian lifestyle after leaving home. It's possible that these may all have been causes or consequences of the family break-up.

Probably though, the departure of Barnabas Mayston Bond, on selling the Hammersmith premises, for a new life overseas now appears to be the more likely catalyst for the loosening of any remaining family ties.

Barnabas Mayston Bond's other lives: Devon

Having routinely searched for the dates of Zoë's parents' deaths, I unexpectedly stumbled upon additional information connected with the West Country. In passing, it's noticeable that Devon does seem to have had a particular pull for the Bonds: in addition to the Devonian location of Walter Tremayne's school (to be detailed shortly), there was a one-time address of Barnabas's sister Mary Patten Bond (see End Note 63). We also saw in Chapter Two that Dr Bond had been a member of the 'Devon' Masonic Lodge in Jullundur, India.

Barnabas Mayston's address at his death on 14 October 1934 was 7 Seymour Road, Newton, Devon. Furthermore, according to the Wills and Probate Register 1934[261] he had previously been living at 20 Stoneyhill, Abbotskerswell, also in Devon. I began to ponder what influences had encouraged this son of Norfolk, erstwhile London doctor, to gravitate south-westwards. I found detail - too remote (even!) for this account - that the family of his maternal grandfather James Patten had origins there.

Barnabas Mayston Bond's other lives: Clapton, London E5

I decided to delve a little deeper into census and other records. As mentioned earlier, curiously I had found no trace of any members of the Bond family in the 1911 census. Checking again, I happened to notice an entry for a Caroline Annie Woods aged 24, who had been born in Bethnal Green, and was working as a live-in servant at Garden Reach, Grove Park Road, Chiswick, some three miles away from the Bond family home. This location may be entirely coincidental, but given that it is arguably within a doctor's catchment area it potentially could have had some relevance as will be

Fig. 26: 41 Glyn Road, Clapton, London E5, 2017. Photo by author.

explored shortly.

The life events of this Caroline Annie, born in Bethnal Green in 1886, can be traced at various points via official records.[262] She had been baptised on 24 October 1886 at St Andrews, Bethnal Green, where her parents James Thomas Woods (a painter) and Caroline Woods were listed as resident at 122 Wilmott Street. In the 1901 census Caroline Annie is recorded as a 14-year-old servant at a house in King Edward's Road, Hackney.

The subsequent 1911 census tells us that the Woods family, with daughter Caroline Annie now in service at Chiswick, had only one of their six living children, Alice, at home, which by then was at 41 Glyn Road, Clapton E5 (see Fig. 26).

Chapter Fourteen

The relevance of this to the Bonds of Leyton may seem unexplained, until the following unexpected information of twenty years further on is taken into consideration.

In the UK Incoming Passenger Lists,[263] an entry shows that the P&O ship *Strathnaver*, having sailed from Adelaide and Brisbane, arrived in London on 22 April 1932. The following two names appear consecutively on the ship's register:

> "Bond, Barnabas M., Physician and Surgeon aged 70
> Bond, Caroline A., Home Duties aged 45"

Both passengers had the intended address of "41 Glyn Road London E5" recorded against their name. Recalling that address as having featured in the 1911 census data in relation to the Woods family, I looked through the Hackney Electoral Registers for each of the years 1925, 1927, 1928, 1929, 1930 and 1932. These all show the residents at 41 Glyn Road E5 to be either or both of James Thomas Woods and Caroline Woods, the afore-mentioned parents of Caroline Annie.

Barnabas Mayston Bond's other lives: Australia

Adding these residential records to the data in the 1932 Passenger Lists mentioned above, it appeared that Barnabas Mayston Bond and Caroline Annie Woods had spent some years in Australia, and were returning, as a couple with the surname Bond, to the Woods' family home. The confirming information was that on Barnabas Mayston's death, probate had been granted at Lewes, Sussex, to his widow Caroline Annie Bond. The terms of the will are not known but Barnabas Mayston Bond had left a total of £2,279 6s. 8d.[264]

I realised that, Barnabas Mayston's marriage to Eliza Josephine Luxon having ended on her 1929 death (detail appears shortly), he had subsequently married Caroline Annie. As we have seen from the census she was formerly a servant and was some twenty-five years his junior. Searching for evidence of the marriage eventually led to an entry in the Australian records.

I found the report of a marriage between Barnabas Mayston Bond and Caroline Annie Woods having taken place on 24 March 1930 in South Australia.[265] They were to live only two further years in Australia, returning, as we have seen, by sea in April 1932 when Barnabas was nearing his seventieth year.

It was even trickier to find out when and how Barnabas and Caroline had each made the original voyage out to Australia from Britain. The last we had heard of Zoë's father was that he sold the Hammersmith home and medical practice in 1919 and was going to France with his then wife, Eliza Josephine, for reasons of her health.[266] There was no indication of how long either of them stayed in France, or indeed whether they ever arrived.

However there is a record[267] of a voyage being made by the White Star Line ship *Ceramic*, which left Liverpool on 21 April 1921 for Capetown, Adelaide, Melbourne and Sydney, with the following-named two passengers on board, on adjacent 'Contract Ticket' numbers in Cabin Class bound for Adelaide and with Australia marked as 'Country of Intended Residence':

> "1329 Bond Mr B. M., Engineer age 25
> 1330 Woods Miss C. A., Domestic age 27".

It is not totally conclusive that this was Barnabas's escape with Miss Woods, since the passenger with Contract Ticket 1329 has no given medical title, is described as an engineer and is rather younger than Zoë's father would have been. But in fact the age given for the Mr B. M. Bond coincides, perhaps eerily, with what would have been Barnabas Mayston's deceased son Hugh Trevor's age, had he lived.

The next-listed passenger's details are a distinct match for Caroline Annie Woods. In the circumstance that there appears to be no trace in UK national records of a 'B. M. Bond' being born in 1896 (the calculated birth date for passenger 1329), and there being no other records of Barnabas Mayston Bond making an antipodean voyage, the coincidence cannot be ignored. Added to that is the circumstantial information that only two months after the date of this outward-bound sea voyage, his daughter Zoë Millicent was at the Kensington Registry Office marrying Oliver Augustus Hart Dyke, with neither Barnabas Mayston nor Eliza Josephine being present.

A search of passport applications[268] for Barnabas Mayston Bond yielded no results. Noting that before the First World War travellers abroad did not need passports, an assumption may also be made that, given Dr Bond had travelled to and from Punjab in the early 1900s, he may have had no difficulty in overseas travel. Even so, the unanswered queries about the precise date and travel route of Barnabas Mayston to Australia are of minor importance, since the records of professional practice that he established in Adelaide from 1924 – 1931[269] provide authoritative confirmation that he was indeed there for some time. His medical practice was listed at the remote village of Mallala and he was appointed also to attend 'Destitute Persons' at Port Gawler.[270]

Why did they come back? The return to England in 1932 by Barnabas and Caroline may have been prompted by Barnabas' health in his elder years, or it could have been for economic reasons.

Eliza Josephine and the Egypt connection

So what had happened to Zoë's mother, Eliza Josephine, in the meantime? The search for answers to this took in further data from shipping records. I found that a Mrs E. J. Bond, aged 66, arrived in London on 9 June 1927 on the P & O *Orama*,[271] having sailed first-class. The ship had come from Brisbane, but would have picked up elsewhere on the way. Mrs Bond's country of permanent residence was given in the ship's record as 'Egypt'.

At first, this traveller may not have seemed a match for Eliza Josephine, but two other facts suggest otherwise. Zoë had noted that her elder brother, Walter Tremayne Bond, settled in Egypt after the First World War.[272] Later he was to become the Joint Manager of the Port Said & Suez Coal Co. Ltd., and in 1941 he received an OBE.[273] It would not be surprising therefore for Eliza Josephine to be staying with her son, but I needed to find clearer evidence of it.

The clue was to be found in the intended address of passenger Mrs E. J. Bond. The ship's register shows that it was '16 Yeomans Row, Brompton Road, London'. This turns out to be the home address[274] of Ernest and Elsie Margaret Lomax. From the evidence of the St Paul's Girl's School archivist, we already know that Elsie Margaret Lomax was Zoë's sister and later we will see the evidence of Elsie's marriage to Ernest. So it seems that Eliza Josephine, apparently having been estranged from Barnabas for an unknown period, was spending her later years living with their adult children.

There was no record to be found however, whether from public data or in Zoë's writings, that Eliza Josephine spent any time in her later years with her youngest daughter, Zoë Millicent. On the contrary, the record of her first-class outgoing voyage from London to Port Said in 1923 indicates that Eliza Josephine may have spent up to four years in Egypt with son Walter Tremayne. The British India line vessel *Morvada's* register for that sailing on 30 August 1923 shows the 62-year-old Eliza Josephine's home address as 25 Comeragh Road W14, but lists her 'Country of Last Residence' as 'Foreign Countries'.[275] This points to the possibility that at some point she had indeed been in France, as Zoë has written.

The later lives of Zoë's Leyton-born siblings

Zoë's brother - Walter Tremayne, the eldest, born in 1889, as we learned earlier, became a successful shipping manager in the Middle East. Walter had been sent to boarding school, possibly even before the Bonds left Leyton, as evidenced in the 1901 census entry for an institution at 98 High Street, Honiton, Devon, that also gave his name, age and birthplace. During the First World War, Walter Tremayne had served as a gunner with the Royal Artillery, enlisting as a private and arriving in Port Said in 1915. He rose through the ranks to a sergeant, and was commissioned as a captain in February 1917. His last record in the army is dated 23 June 1923, at Alexandria.[276]

In 1919, he became a member, like his father Barnabas Mayston, of the United Grand Lodge of England Freemasons, and was part of the Norfolk branch.[277] He was listed there with the rank of captain, and resident at Port Said. The likelihood is that his marriage to Evelyn May Hardy, who was some fourteen years his junior, took place in Port Said, since there are no UK records to be found of a marriage between the two. Disappointingly, the pertinent Port Said records are not available for internet searching.[278] But more significantly there is a record of a child Evelyn May Hardy travelling with one Elizabeth Anne Hardy on the merchant ship *Arabistan* to Port Said, departing from Manchester on 9 November 1909.[279] This supports Evelyn's 1903 date of birth and what can be assumed about her presence in Port Said.

Walter Tremayne lived until 1958. Evelyn May's date of birth can be corroborated as 1903 from an inscription much later dedicated to her and Walter Tremayne:[280]

> "Walter Tremayne Bond OBE 1889 – 1958
> Evelyn his wife 1903 – 1991"

Walter Tremayne and Evelyn May are to be found on various UK Passenger Lists of sea voyages travelling between the Middle East and England, together with their son Basil Tremayne (born in Port Said in 1926) and daughter Diane Josephine during the 1920s – 1940s. Diane's second name was perhaps in remembrance of her grandmother Eliza Josephine Bond.

Through his residence overseas, Walter had proved useful and loyal to his sister Zoë, in particular being a source of mulberry plant exporter contacts, as noted earlier. Interestingly, Walter and Evelyn's son Basil followed in his grandfather Barnabas Mayston's footsteps and took up a career in medicine, working as a GP in Penrhyn, Cornwall.[281]

Zoë's sister - Elsie Margaret married Ernest P. Lomax at Kensington in the summer of 1921 as we have noted, only one day after her sister Zoë's first marriage into the Hart Dyke family. The Lomaxes lived in West London at first, with the address of 28 Wyndham Street, Bryanston Square, London W1 in 1924, but are later to be found on the Finsbury (Islington, London) Electoral Register for 1938 having property at 156 Farringdon Road and at Egerton Place Studios, 16 Yeomans Road, London SW3. Possibly the Farringdon Road address, a commercial area of London, was in respect of Ernest's business activity which we know was design. We know from Elsie Margaret's letter to St Paul's Girls' School (See Appendix 4) that contact was maintained between the two sisters in their adult lives. Elsie was to die in the same year, 1975, as Zoë.

Zoë's eldest sister - Sylvia Christine, as noted in Chapter Five, had married William Wilson Simpson at St John the Baptist church on 7 September 1918. She died in 1955, this being earlier than any of her siblings. It seems that she had the least contact of her siblings with Zoë.

The patchy and uneven pictures from public records

The lives of Barnabas Mayston, Zoë Millicent and Walter Tremayne are available to us to view through the prism of public record-keeping from the late nineteenth century onwards, not least as a result of the paths chosen by those individuals in terms of professions and upwardly-mobile marriage. In contrast, there has been little to follow up on the lives of Elsie Margaret and her sister Sylvia Christine. Partly this may be explained by the fact that as women, they featured less often in the public records of the first half of the twentieth century.

There are interesting gender, age and class aspects illustrated variously by the uneven pattern of data left behind. As mentioned in relation to Eliza Josephine in Chapter

Two, the Representation of the People Act 1918 had extended the vote to women with particular property or marriage qualifications. However it still excluded women such as Elsie Margaret and Sylvia Christine, since the qualifying minimum age was 30 years. Accordingly these sisters probably did not become eligible to vote until their middle age. Sylvia Christine's first record on the Hammersmith & Fulham Electoral Register was in 1933, even though she had married William Wilson Simpson in 1918 and he had been included in the said register at that constant address throughout the 1920s.[282]

The last days of Barnabas Mayston, Eliza Josephine and Zoë

While Zoë's writings give little indication of contact with her siblings after she joined the Hart Dyke family, the above paragraphs shed some light on what links there were. We have seen that in the years after the First World War the Bond family became significantly dispersed, with Barnabas going to live in Australia, Eliza Josephine possibly to France thence Egypt, and the offspring going their separate ways.

As mentioned earlier, Eliza Josephine had left her estate to Zoë's two sisters only. She died, recorded as wife of Barnabas Mayston Bond,[283] at Southsea House, Harrow Road, West Dorking, Surrey, on Christmas Day 1929, leaving £432.13s.4d.[284]

Only three months later Barnabas married his sweetheart Caroline Annie Woods, their liaison having already lasted at least a decade and possibly up to eighteen years, although there is no precise evidence.

Barnabas's own death back in England in 1934 was announced in Australia:

> "BOND – On the 14th October, at Newton Abbot, Barnabas Mayston Bond, M.R.C.S. L.R.C.P., the beloved husband of Caroline Annie Bond, 20 Stoneyhill, Abbottskerswell, Devon, aged 73."[285]

The question arises as to who, in Australia, would have wanted to know about his demise, given that both Barnabas and Caroline Annie had returned to the UK, as is evident also from the death notice. I could find no answer. But searching the internet, I found traces of descendant families with connections to the Bonds. Dr Bond's second marriage seems to have been unknown to these sources until his death record was accessed by them. It appears therefore that Barnabas Mayston's Australian existence was kept from the wider family. An unchecked report in *The Times* newspaper, states that Barnabas Mayston Bond was buried back at Alburgh Church in Norfolk on 17 October 1934. This is still to be verified.

Eliza Josephine's personal legacy in 1929 of £432.13s.4d. points towards her having separate financial affairs from those of Barnabas even though there had been no divorce. She may have received some proceeds from Barnabas's sale of the Hammersmith premises or it may have been her own family money from Cornwall.

Caroline Annie's long wait to marry Barnabas was rewarded by her appointment as executor of the £2,279.6s.8d inheritance from the Bond estate, a good amount for the 1930s. However she had a long widowhood ahead of her, and would survive until 28 September 1973.[286] Having moved to the south coast at some point, Caroline died at Hove, Sussex. She had obtained probate for Barnabas, as noted earlier, at nearby Lewes.

Following Barnabas's death Caroline Annie had returned to Australia at least once: embarking by sea from London on the *Orontes* of the Orient shipping line on 14th December 1946 bound for Melbourne.[287] She later disembarked in London on MV *Empire Star* of the Blue Star Line on 24 October 1947[288] aged 60, with the Woods family address, still 41 Glyn Road, Clapton, London, marked as her destination. Curiously, the records show that she had started the voyage in Wellington, New Zealand. Caroline Annie's links with Australia and New Zealand have not been further researched at this stage, but indications such as the newspaper advert of Barnabas's death, and the post-war journeys, point to the existence of some important connections for her there.

As regards Zoë herself, she died at a nursing home on 12 February 1975, leaving £2,690.[289] [290]

Life patterns

At the beginning of writing this biography, indeed well into halfway through it, I had no idea that there would be such a similar direction of life for Zoë our protagonist and her father Barnabas Mayston. They both achieved happiness and fulfilment later in life with a partner who had not been the first. The transition from one partner to the second involved for each of them major changes to livelihood arrangements.

They both achieved much in their time. They each kept secrets about significant aspects of their lives from their descendants. It remains unknown as to which point in time was the last one that they shared together.

The Bonds' links with Leyton

The Bond family's link with Leyton is transient, but I have tried to identify an arguable and traceable logic, connected with Barnabas Mayston's career progression imperatives, for his original choice of this growing suburb and, subsequently, the circumstances in which he moved the family away.

In her writings, Zoë chose to ignore the location of her start in life. Although her grandson Tom didn't challenge what Zoë had written in that respect, it was clear from my conversation with Guy Hart Dyke that the descendant family is aware of the Leyton origins. In the meantime it has fallen to your author, in this work, to confirm that Zoë Millicent Hart Dyke (née Bond) was indeed a daughter of Leyton.

Chapter Fifteen: What to make of Zoë

A variety of common threads run through our story.

Mulberry trees and silk

Firstly the mulberry tree blossoms as a central feature of Zoë's life, albeit it as a means to an end. Everywhere that she lived, studied or worked was blessed with a mulberry tree or there was a connection to one nearby. She was born in a house where a black mulberry tree stood in the garden, the two houses in Poole were not far away from similar specimens, the school in Hammersmith had a mulberry tree in the grounds and at Saumur, France, she discovered where to obtain mulberry leaves and whom to deploy to pick them, as she also did when living in Earl's Court. Moving to Leatherhead imposed a bit of a gap, but that was resolved swiftly. She sought mulberry trees from among her contacts, whether odd-balls, socialites or 'top-drawer' nobility.

Once she was at Lullingstone there was nothing to stop this pre-occupation with the food source of her beloved silkworms. The silk-worm fascination evidently developed into an obsession, driving her to do anything and everything possible to obtain the much-needed mulberry leaves. When even the impact of hostile Second World War action did not destroy her silk-worm stock completely she deployed the billeted soldiers as farm labourers on the mulberry plantations and as carers for the arthropod livestock. She was swiftly able to resume sericulture enthusiastically afterwards. Zoë was, supremely, a highly specialised and creative master technician of sericulture.

Business and feminism

Secondly it's a woman's story. Through her book, Zoë has given us a chronicle that is an account of a feminine-dominated business. Zoë has illustrated her book proudly with images of mid-twentieth-century women at work on the enterprise It shows how she employed women in the skilled but sometimes unpleasant jobs of nurturing the worms and reeling the raw silk, while the men were allocated the semi- and unskilled work on her land. However Zoë would subsume any ideological idea she might have had about this when the occasion demanded. An example of such was the change of arrangements during the Second World War, when the Land Girls, possibly the marchers on parade in Fig. 21, were deployed on the mulberries while the soldiers were in the hatching, rearing and cocoon-spinning quarters.

We have examined reference to the possible influences on Zoë's attitudes, ranging from ostentatiousness in Soho through high culture in Knightsbridge to the more subdued splendour of Scotland. Mostly the key characters are women, and in each case Zoë exhibits pride in recounting the tales of her times with them and what she learned from them.

By contrast the men that she mentions, whether Gustav Holst, her father or the hapless Leatherhead baker, are regarded with varying degrees of condescending impatience, the exception being Major R. Field Bibb, to whom Zoë listened closely and was willing to learn about the commercial aspects of her great sericulture experiment. Ultimately he became her final life partner, although as we learned legally he never abandoned his own wife.

Zoë herself gave the background to her 'feminist' rationale in a speech at the *Home Life Exhibition* in Brighton, 1938. The word 'feminist' is given in inverted commas here since Zoë did not profess to be one. She explained:

> "If a woman tries to run a business, people have three explanations for her peculiar action. Firstly, she is doing it to support a family, or perchance a drunken male relative; secondly she has been crossed in love, and is trying to forget the distressing incident by hard work; thirdly, she is a mannish type – all tweeds, collar and tie. What people seem to forget, or perhaps do not understand, is that some women like business for its own sake, and enjoy it tremendously; I come under this category."[291]

Looking at each of Zoë's criteria in turn; it's easy to agree firstly that she wasn't effective in financially supporting her family and that this was not really one of her aims. As to whether she would have considered herself 'mannish' or not, we can only hazard a guess at a couple of the images that have survived. Her portrait at the beginning of this book does indeed show her in a stout tweed-type suit. On the other hand while the image of her riding a scooter with sidecar in 1956 (Fig. 20) indicates that she was ready for anything with her high-heels speaking of her feminine side. Her reference to a 'mannish' woman perhaps alluded to her unconventional mother-in-law, Lady Caroline Emily Hart Dyke, as pictured in Fig. 15.

Although she claims it to be the case, Zoë was patently not in business for its own sake: the business was the way in which she tried to turn a personal passion, an obsession, into a sustainable going concern. Some might say that this is what a business is, but the essential extra ingredient of making a profit was not Zoë's forte: she constantly sought other ways of enabling the business to exist, always seeking practical and technical solutions, sometimes unorthodox ones and leaning heavily on the status afforded by the Hart Dyke family and royal patronage.

Social class

Thirdly, as hinted at in my introduction, it's a tale of eccentricity and social mobility within twentieth-century British class structure. Zoë had an innate ruthlessness that enabled her to go for the main chance despite, or maybe because of, a lack of academic prowess. She successfully made the transitions from newly-urbanised Leyton eventually to a mediaeval-age castle in Kent by fully utilising the social and educational advantages that her parents had bestowed on her. She trod on the toes, if not the backs, of others on the way.

Characters in her family background, both paternal and maternal, show her childhood influences to be those of go-ahead, ambitious people. The story also shows how the inheritance of money played a key factor in enabling Zoë and the people around her to make significant and life-affecting decisions. Although Zoë missed out on the financial inheritance of both her parents they ensured that she benefited from the Bond inheritance during her childhood. She then moved into a different seat of wealth – a titled family with inherited property albeit suffering from liquidity limitations. This position gave her access, as we have seen, to socialites, artists, industrialists and nobility.

Class and influence were prominent aspects in Zoë's view of the world. Grandson Tom recounted:

> "When she wanted egg supplies or advice on the practical or commercial side of silk production, she would skip off to Milan and gaily secure introductions to the people in the industry who mattered… Grandma Zoë always seemed to know of a little man somewhere who would fall under her spell and get things sorted. She'd write shamelessly to an ambassador she vaguely knew here, or to a military attaché she'd once met there, and she usually secured the help she wanted."[292]

Zoë had certainly learned how to utilise the connections to advance her aesthetic and artisan skills, and her fascination with innovation, not to mention novelty.

Attitudes and achievements

To be fair to Zoë, her book was never intended to be a complete autobiography, but there may well be perfectly natural reasons for her choices of what to include or what to omit. She wrote it when there would still be twenty-five years more to live, so we do not have access to any reflections she may have had in her senior years.

The failure in her book to mention the Bonds' first ten years of family life in Leyton may be attributed to its perceived irrelevance to Zoë, or it could be that 'Dorsetshire'[293] was seen as more suitable to her subsequent status. The failure to mention her parents' lack of involvement in either of her weddings and the subsequent years without their support as her own young family grew, perhaps can be seen as indicative of a stoic, stiff-upper-lip outlook in that era.

The main benefit that she drew from her beginnings was the ambition and confidence as a woman to attempt the commercial-scale sericulture experiment. The pinnacle that she reached, from her point of view, was being appointed to supply silk for the coronations and royal weddings of the mid-twentieth century. Even though she was rarely granted direct contact with the royal family, she encouraged her employees with her own sycophantic admiration and deference for the monarchs and their descendants. To quote one of the final paragraphs of Zoë's autobiography,[294] which concludes the episode in which she had sent the silk and angora bonnet to Buckingham Palace, she writes in unmistakably British mid-century loyal tones:

"Yesterday the anxiously-awaited letter arrived. H.R.H. graciously accepted the bonnet … when the news spread through the Silk Farm, enthusiasm was unbounded, everybody hugged everybody else, and when a group of visitors arrived to see over the Farm, they were immediately told the joyful tidings, and they cheered and cheered again, so that the echoes scurried through every nook and cranny of Lullingstone until it seemed as though the house itself shook with laughter."

The wartime years apart, and taking into account what living conditions were like for anyone at the time, Zoë as an adult was not directly touched by surrounding economic hardship or austerity. Her privileged position allowed her to live comfortably, travel extensively and be entertained. But there is no denying that she threw her whole self and effort into what she did, and expected others to work just as hard.

It is left to other commentators including, ironically, a press report from Australia in 1947, to boast of Zoë's export undertakings, namely that: she directed the generation by silkworms of eight million cocoons which were exported variously to Australia, Bahamas, United States and Denmark in the ensuing fifteen years.[295] It is notable that the cocoon exports were made post-war when Lullingstone Silk Farm Ltd came under more stringent business management than the single-handed pioneering by Zoë in the nineteen-thirties when her effort was restricted to the production of the silk yarn.

How Zoë has been viewed by history so far

While it would seem that Zoë's practical abilities and non-conformity had been the immediate attraction for Oliver Augustus, it was her ambition and determination that enabled her to invent a unique place inside the formalised structure of his establishment family. Her unconventional streak and rebellious nature, both of which she traces back to her childhood, also led her out of a decade of dutiful domestic and maternal confinement into the innovation, enterprise and flamboyance of the 1930s.

Zoë's accolades, such as they were, were received in her lifetime but, poignantly, she lived to see her actual creation, in the shape of fully operational silk farming and processing, decline. While her social networking genius and assertive attitudes got Zoë into some scrapes, they had also led her into glamorous and artistic niches of the fashionable middle and upper classes in the interwar years.

Although she became a member of the Association of Women Executives,[296] and as noted earlier, received a silver medal from the RSA, Zoë hasn't yet been celebrated by her school, she didn't make it into the archives of women's achievements of the 1930s,[297] nor has she gone down in history in the way that her friends and fellow high-flyers have done. Essentially she was a technician rather than artist and sadly this has often been an aspect of human endeavour unfairly unrecognised in British society.[298]

She was undoubtedly a perfectionist and attained exalted levels of quality in her chosen field. It is certainly time for Zoë to be more widely recognised, given her singular achievements.

As Tom admits, his grandmother was:

> " ... truly inspiring" and "a veritable human dynamo."[299]

The *Oxford Biography* records that Zoë's silk farm at Lullingstone was:

> " ... large, internationally famous and commercial".[300]

A more recent authority[301] describes Zoë's achievement in British sericulture as:

> "The most successful enterprise of the past four hundred years".

An even later evaluation of Zoë's achievement assesses further that Lullingstone was:

> "England's only successful twentieth-century silk farm."[302]

The main legacy: at Lullingstone Castle

A search on the internet for 'Lullingstone Silk Farm' now produces www.lullingstonecastle.co.uk/lullingstone-silk-farm as the first option to view. Zoë's descendants have created a fresh look at her achievements, tempting visitors to Lullingstone Castle and the World Garden to see for themselves aspects of the silk farm heritage not forgetting the mulberry plants propagated from Zoë's originals.[303]

It would seem that Zoë's time has come round at last.

Unravelling the Yarn

SELECTED BIBLIOGRAPHY AND REFERENCES 1:

Books

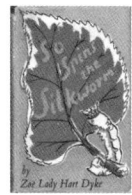

So Spins the Silkworm, Zoë Lady Hart Dyke, Rockliff, London, 1949

An Englishman's Home, Tom Hart Dyke, Bantam Press, London, 2007. Tom Hart Dyke is a grandson of Zoë.

Lullingstone Castle and the World Garden, introduction by Guy Hart Dyke, Tony Russell Associates, Gloucestershire, 2008. Guy Hart Dyke was born in 1928 as Oliver Guy, son of Zoe and Oliver Augustus Hart Dyke. info@lullingstonecastle.co.uk.

Lullingstone Silk Farm 1932 – 1955, Zoë Lady Hart Dyke. Self-published, printed at Dimond & Co. Ltd, Dartford, Kent.

SELECTED BIBLIOGRAPHY AND REFERENCES 2:
Papers

'Silkworms in England Spin for the Queen', John E. H. Nolan, in *National Geographic,* 1953, pages 689 – 704.
14 - page feature including several photographs of Zoë's enterprise

Journal of the Royal Society of Arts, 25 December 1936

SELECTED BIBLIOGRAPHY AND REFERENCES 3:

Extracts

Time Magazine, Monday, 4 January 1937: "Science: Lady's Worms"

> "In England there is only one producer of raw silk on a practical scale, and she is Lady Millicent Zoe Hart Dyke, nee Bond, wife of Engineer Sir Oliver Hamilton Augustus Hart Dyke, Bart. At present her small industry is enjoying brisk business, for the new Queen and the Duchesses of Gloucester and Kent have patriotically-commanded that their coronation gowns be made of British silk. .. The Dyke silk is grown at Lullingstone Castle, Kent, rushed to Macclesfield (neckties) to be "thrown" (twisted for proper thread thickness), then to Braintree to be boiled and dyed... "

Oxford Dictionary of National Biography, John Martin, published online, September 2004

> "Dyke [née Bond], (Millicent) Zoë, Lady Dyke (1896-1975), pioneer of British sericulture, was born on 6 February 1896 at 9 Manor Road, Leyton, Essex, the daughter of Barnabas Mayston Bond ..."

The Telegraph 22 April 2011

> "The fabric for the dress was woven at Winterthur Silks Limited, Dunfermline, in the Canmore factory, using silk that had come from Chinese silkworms at Lullingstone Castle."

The Gravesend Reporter 5 January 2011

> "Anya, who is the sister of Lullingstone's World Garden Creator and Times columnist Tom Hart Dyke added: "It's a shame that there isn't any silk production in the country any more, but it's just not a financially viable business."

A film available online, dated 1948
www.britishpathe.com/video/silkworms-receive-blessing/query/Lullingstone

> "Procession of men and women walking from Lullingstone Castle to St. Botolph's Church in Farningham, Kent. Back shot of procession entering church. Side shot of procession entering church. Close up shot of Lady Hart-Dyke entering church. Panning shot of church window. People walking to seats. Close up shot of the wheel. Close up shot of the cocoons. Close up shot of the eggs. Women walking to camera. Back shot of girls handing silk to priest. Close up shot of the Priest, Reverend Hal Jefferson, with silk. Close up shot of the women praying. Shot of the village."

Selected Bibliography and References

Unidentified newspaper, 26 June 1936[304]

"Silkworm's Half-Mile Thread: Queen Mary's Visit to Kent Farm.
Queen Mary this afternoon viewed a silkworm farm which Lady Hart Dyke is operating in Lullingstone Park, near Eynsford, in Kent. The farm, started as an experiment four years ago, is expected to produce some 1,500lb. of fine pure silk from cocoons this year. The inspection was of a private character, but the people of Eynsford and other villages who had heard that the Queen was to visit the district gathered on the sides of the roads and also in the grounds of the beautiful park to offer a quiet welcome to her Majesty. At Lullingstone House the Queen was received by Sir Oliver and Lady Hart Dyke.

Queen Mary, who was deeply interested, was shown all the processes which are carried through the farm. The eggs from which the silkworms are bred are imported during the winter from Turkey, France, China, Japan, and India, and are kept in cold storage until the mulberry trees are in leaf. Mulberry leaves are essential to feed the worms in their larval stage. At Lullingstone the eggs are hatched in incubators which can provide controlled temperatures. The Queen saw an incubator room in which were about 500,000 eggs obtained from France, Turkey, and China. Lady Hart Dyke carries her process through to the reeling of the silk. Spinning and weaving are entrusted to commercial experts, but fabrics which were put before the Queen were proof of the quality of the silk which is produced on the farm. Her Majesty proceeded by car to the gardens adjoining the house where mulberry bushes and trees have been planted to provide the necessary food.

These, however, are still young, and an infant industry of Kent is a present mainly dependant on mulberry leaves supplied by owners of trees who are interested in the scheme. Lady Hart Dyke needs more of these leaves, and would welcome notification from those who can send them so that arrangements can be made for an even distribution of arrivals. Before leaving for Buckingham Palace her Majesty expressed the pleasure she had derived from her afternoon. Contingents of the Dartford Rural District Council Fire Brigade were formed up on the lawn of the house as Queen Mary drove away."

SELECTED BIBLIOGRAPHY AND REFERENCES 4:

Additional works by Zoë Lady Hart Dyke

Silk Farm: The Wonderful Story Of Silk And How You Can Produce It At Home Told For The Children By Zoe Lady Hart Dyke. Millicent Zoë Hart Dyke, Westchester, 1948. This used (coloured-in)! book has been offered for sale on Ebay, second-hand, since at least 18 May 2015, first priced at £270, now down to £115.

The Tale of Sebastian the Silkworm by Marjorie Dawson (Illustrator), Zoë Lady Hart Dyke (Author)
Perry Son & Lack, Ltd. Lowfield Works, Dartford, 1936.
Available second-hand from Amazon for £49.99, consists of 16 pages.

Lullingstone Silk Farm 1932 – 47
A booklet by Zoë Lady Hart Dyke
Image unattributed from internet

Lullingstone Silk Farm 1932 – 1945
A booklet by Zoë Lady Hart Dyke
Image unattributed from internet

SELECTED BIBLIOGRAPHY AND REFERENCES 5:

Lullingstone Silk Farm at Ayot St Lawrence: visitor brochures, courtesy of Mill Green Museum, Hatfield, Herts.

Brochure 1957

Leaflet 1970

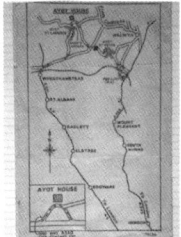

Map 1957

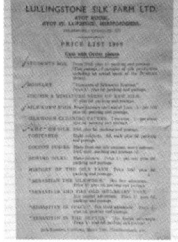

Price list 1969

Undated brochure

Unravelling the Yarn

APPENDICES

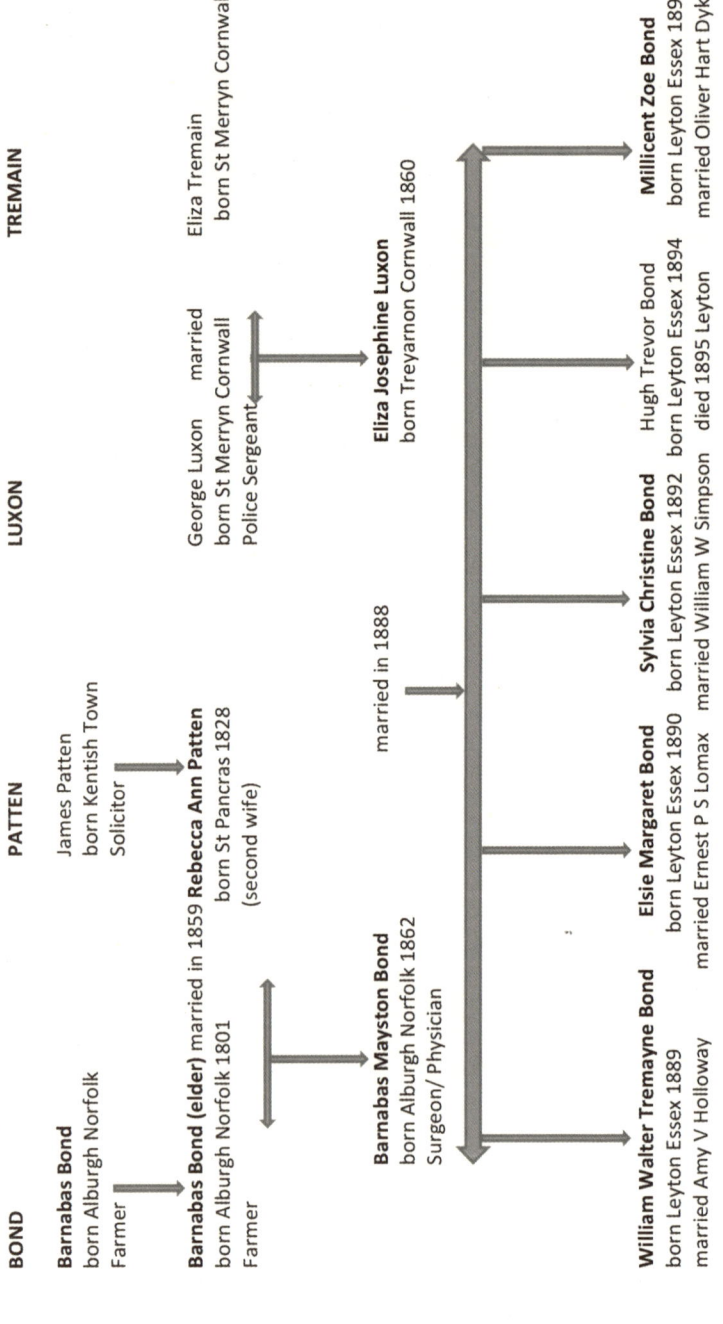

APPENDIX 1 The Bonds: an outline ancestry - diagrammatic view

APPENDIX 2A The Hart Dykes: an outline ancestry – diagrammatic view

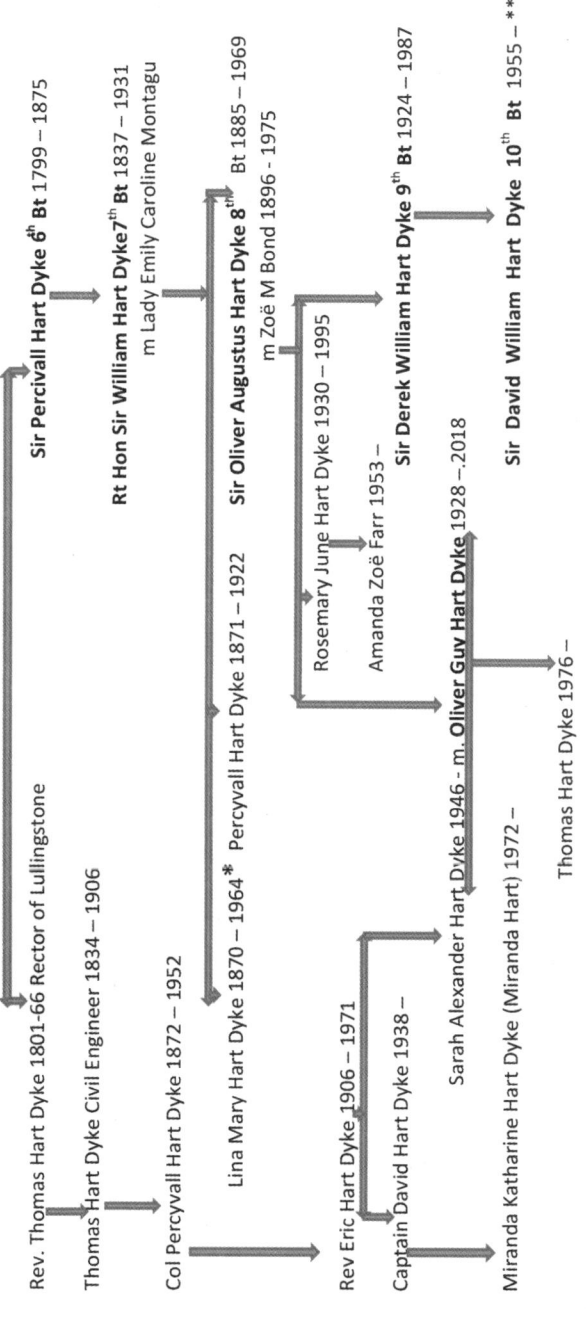

Please note: this diagram does not include all spouses or descendants, siblings may not be in birth order but reflect rules of inheritance.
*Mrs Crivellari, Zoë's sponsor   ** No issue: An *Englishman's Home*, Tom Hart Dyke, 2007, p 138

APPENDIX 2B Dates of Hart Dyke Baronetcies

Ordinal	Name and title	From: death of predecessor	Until: own death
5th	Sir Percyvall Hart Dyke (born 1767)	22 November 1831	4 August 1846
6th	Sir Percyvall Hart Dyke (born 1799)	4 August 1846	12 November 1875
7th	Rt Hon. Sir William Hart Dyke (born 1837)	12 November 1875	3 July 1931
8th	Sir Oliver Hamilton Augustus Hart Dyke (born 1885)	3 July 1931	9 July 1969
9th	Sir Derek William Hart Dyke (born 1924)	9 July 1969	14 September 1987
10th	Sir David William Hart Dyke (born 1955)	14 September 1987	

APPENDIX 2C: Baronetcies and inheritance

Baronets (Bt) are classified as 'titled gentry' and have a historical status going back to the granting of baronetcies by James 1 of England. They pass on the status to the eldest son. Note that the daughters of baronets do not have the opportunity to inherit the title. The equal status of females to succeed to the United Kingdom throne[305] does not apply in the families of dukes, earls or baronets. Attempts to redress that have so far been unsuccessful.[306] Feminism has not yet triumphed over class in this matter.

An heir apparent is the person whose right to succeed cannot be defeated. An heir presumptive on the other hand, is one whose right to succeed stands to change if other events advance a different descendant's position. This has happened more than once in the Hart Dyke family, most significantly here in 1922 when Percyvall Hart Dyke, eldest son of Right Hon Sir William 7th Baronet, died without leaving any direct heirs. This gave rise to Percyvall's younger brother Oliver Augustus Hamilton Hart Dyke becoming the heir apparent from that date and thus inheriting the title of 8th Baronet on the eventual death in 1931 of their father.

Inheriting the title is not necessarily accompanied by the ownership of any property. Currently the 10th Baronetcy is held by Sir David Hart Dyke who remains resident in Canada, and what is left of the actual Lullingstone estate remaining under the responsibility of his nephew Oliver Guy Hart Dyke.

A baronet is known as 'Sir' and the wife of a baronet assumes the title of 'Lady'. A 'Lady' whose married status in the family ceases (for instance through divorce or widowhood) must relinquish the word 'Lady' as the first word in her title, but may use it in a rearranged order. This explains the convention "Zoë Lady Hart Dyke" from 1944 onwards, and also distinguishes our heroine from other Lady Hart Dykes designated in her lifetime:[307] there were to be two of them.[308]

APPENDIX 3A 9 Manor Road, Leyton

Zoë's birthplace

Fig. 27: 9 Manor Road, Leyton, E10, front aspect, Barnabas Mayston Bond's first medical practice, the Bonds' family home. Photo by author, 2015.

APPENDIX 3B

9 Manor Road mulberry - photograph

Fig. 28: Mulberry tree at 9 Manor Road, with Ivan, photo by author, 1977

This black mulberry tree had two principal branches upwards and there is a lower one that spread along the ground (behind Ivan on the slide!). The lifeless trunk to the right was part of an apple tree.

In the background are the Lea Hall Gardens flats, built by Waltham Forest Council in the 1960s on the site of Second World War bomb-damaged Victorian houses in Lea Hall Road.

APPENDIX 3C

9 Manor Road mulberry - letter
Letter dated 22 August 1975 from RHS re mulberry tree at 9 Manor Road

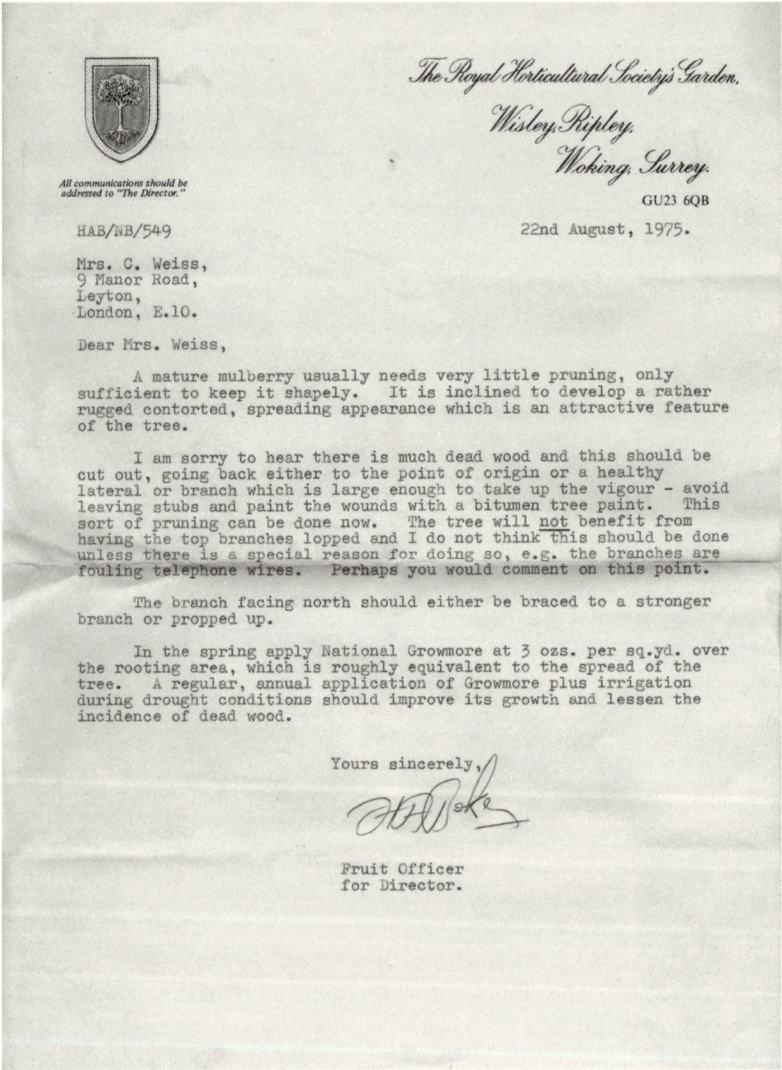

Fig. 29: Letter to author from Royal Horticultural Society, 1975, answering author's request for guidance on care for the mulberry tree.

APPENDIX 3D: Early house numbering in Manor Road

The original Manor Road addresses in documents relating to the Bonds lack number consistency: the birth of the Bonds' firstborn, Walter, was recorded in 1889 at No. 7, whereas Millicent Zoë's birth in 1896 was at No. 9, the latter concurring with the medical registration of Dr Bond of 1895. Interestingly the 1890 *Kelly's Directory*[309] had listed Dr Bond's premises as being at No. 7.

Because such inconsistency is not unusual, I make the assumption that the Bonds' only residence was the building that continues to be numbered as No. 9, originally known as "Treyarnon", and that perhaps it briefly became No. 7 for some administrative reason.

APPENDIX 3E Mulberry trees and Manor Road, Leyton

Leyton Grange

Potentially interesting local connections to all things silk in the seventeenth century came to light as I re-read *The Grange*,[310] David Ian Chapman's history of the Manor in Leyton! I discovered that the Secretary of State to King James I (the monarch who imported mulberries and had them planted for the purpose of starting British silk industry) was Sir Thomas Lake the elder,[311] whose son, Sir Thomas Lake the younger, sold his holding of the whole Manor of Leyton in 1649, including the original Manor House, gatehouse and gardens to three gentlemen. One of these was David Gansel the elder, from a Huguenot family of silk-weavers who had arrived in England in 1684. He bought one part of the Leyton Manor holding in 1703 and also acquired a second part in 1710. David Gansel the younger then had built there a magnificent mansion and formal garden as a replacement for Leyton Grange. The site of the impressive complex is beneath the present day Grange Park Road. Chapman adds:

> "The furthest part of the garden is the boundary formed by what is today the descriptive Park Road."[312]

This would be about thirty metres from the site of the Manor Road mulberry. Interestingly though, in the article 'Low Layton Historical Report' in the St Mary's [Leyton] Parish Magazine of 1924,[313] the Vicar of the time notes:

> " ... the site [of The Leyton Grange] is now somewhere in the neighbourhood of Grange Park and Manor Roads."

There are mentions by Chapman of lime trees and chestnuts in the extensive grounds of The Grange. But the idea does suggest itself, given the ownership history, that some of the trees shown on maps of the estate perhaps might have been mulberries. The Manor Road mulberry, unless it was the result of propagation of this pervasive species[314] could even be an indication of the northern extent of the boundary of The Grange. Further research is earmarked for the future house history of 9 Manor Road!

Unravelling the Yarn

Locally surviving mulberries

Surviving mulberry trees in Britain all owe their existence to having being within the purview of significant buildings, rather than being found in the wild forests. There are two surviving mulberries local to Manor Road. Firstly, the black mulberry tree mentioned in the Introduction (see Figs. 2 and 3) which now has the address of Gainsborough Road, Leytonstone, began life in the grounds of the eighteenth-century Buxton family's Leytonstone House.[315]

The other survivor is a white mulberry tree, at The Old Dispensary, Stratford, London, E15, built circa 1700,[316] now with the address of 30 Romford Road. Sadly the tree has been severely pollarded in order to squeeze into its reduced surroundings. (Fig. 30).[317]

Fig. 30: Mulberry at The Old Dispensary (c1700) Stratford, E15.
Photo by author, 2017.

APPENDIX 4

EXTRACTS FROM *PAULINA*, ST PAUL'S GIRLS' SCHOOL ALUMNAE JOURNAL
Extract 1

July, 1935. DEAR EDITOR,—

It must be confessed I approach this letter with a certain feeling of trepidation. To write about the work of another Paulina has its pitfalls, and, one is within such easy reach of the aggrieved one should misstatements be made! Perhaps if I mention how the idea of this work first started, and give but a brief broad outline of her job, it will suffice to show the problems, hopes, and enthusiasm of an Old Paulina.

There are a number of us who remember Zoe Bond, now the wife of Sir Oliver Hart Dyke, Bart. Zoe's life is a fairly busy one keeping a vigilant eye on the upbringing of her three children, and taking a not inactive part in things political, charitable, and social, she yet finds the time to give serious attention to largescale experiments in silkworm culture. The main object of her work in these experiments is to discover whether it be possible to revive and maintain silkworm culture as a paying commercial proposition in the Home Country. Some of us in our youth may have kept silkworms, and one wonders with what degree of popularity this hobby was viewed at home. During her years at school, Zoe heralded every approaching summer by staggering home with a very large cardboard box crammed to the brim with ravenous, wriggling silkworms. Possibly it was her intense application to school work that prevented her from giving sufficient attention to the commissariat of her "pets" for, like most hungry creatures, they wandered afield in search of food. Not everyone is drawn towards the handling of silkworms, and when Zoe's horde swarmed from their nominal home, the greenhouse, into the dining-room, her relatives shivered with suppressed rage whilst they picked the crawling things from carpet, table legs, chair-backs, and even the parrot's cage. But from these small and far from applauded efforts may spring a new home industry, employing British labour.

It is now four years since Zoe first commenced to think seriously of "home-grown" silk. Her idea of carrying out silkworm culture under the auspices of such unreliable and "shaky" weather as our English summer was met with some amusement and many dismal predictions. But all this sound and wise advice acted as spurs, not brakes, to Zoe's ambition. Her experiments and observations led her to discover some all-important and vital facts. What breeds—from the many different breeds of silkworms—are best adapted to our variable climate, how to avoid or check the numerous diseases this worm is heir to, and which particular mulberry leaf is most suitable for the ultimate production of really good strong silk.

Perhaps the most heartening event during all this period of arduous work was the verdict pronounced on her last year's crop of silk. Zoe sent specimens of this raw material to a well-known laboratory in Italy, and the Italian experts reported " perfect on all points," giving full details as to its fitness to vie with the best silk produced in their own country.

English dyers also were encouraging in their report, stating the silk had stood certain tests well and taken the dyes very satisfactorily. Nor have the English weavers been lacking in giving the right stimulus, they have bought up this season's "crop", although some time must elapse before the exact amount yielded is ascertained. This year sees certain extensions in the silkworm culture. An entire wing of Lullingstone Castle (the Kentish home of the Hart Dykes) has been fitted up for the purpose of hatching and rearing over half-a-million of these useful little creatures. A small staff of girls, supervised by Zoe, are kept busy all day, and every day, cleaning and feeding these worms. The silkworm is a voracious eater, and, with the exception of the four short periods given to "moulting" it never ceases to devour fresh mulberry leaves until the moment arrives for this little creature to perform one of Nature's miracles—spinning the cocoon from a single unbroken thread of silk, nearly half-a-mile in length. On account of the very late and severe frost experienced in early June this year, the thousands of especially selected mulberry bushes, planted in a corner of the Deer Park, received a serious setback. Ex-soldiers were called upon to search far and wide for mulberry trees, and with the aid of kind friends, and complete strangers, owning such trees, a famine in this valuable foodstuff was averted.

This venture has awakened an appreciable amount of public interest. People have written from almost every part of the British Isles asking for particulars and in what way they can further the scheme of the production of silk in this country. Zoe in return has offered every encouragement to those definitely keen on the subject. She has given lectures, demonstrations, supplied women's institutes, schools, etc., with millions of seed (i.e., silkworm eggs), and thousands of mulberry bushes, besides promising to buy the cocoons from those people who desire to find a market for them.

Yours, etc. MARGARET LOMAX.

Howard Bailes, School Archivist at St Paul's Girls' School has identified Margaret Lomax as being a sister of Zoë. Born in 1890, Elsie Margaret was six years the senior.

Extract 2

1968
ZOE HART DYKE AND LULLINGSTONE SILK FARM

On Saturday, June 8th, a party of 31 Old Paulinas and friends, members of the Social Section of the League, paid a visit to Zoe Lady Hart Dyke (Zoe Bond) at Ayot House, Ayot St. Lawrence. Zoe opened the farm especially for us and from the moment of her warm greeting to her cheerful farewell, we were royally entertained. Zoe had kept silk worms since she was four years old and after rearing her children returned to her early hobby. The farm, the only one in Europe, was started in Surrey, moved after fourteen years to Lullingstone Castle in Kent and finally settled in Hertfordshire in 1957. The main problem was to ensure a good supply of mulberry leaves as five tons are needed to feed 250,000 silk worms. This is now solved and the farm flourishes and produces silk for many important people and occasions. Eggs are imported from Japan every second year to prevent inbreeding and these Asian worms spin white silk as opposed to European worms which produce yellow cocoons. In a rearing room, we were shown the complete life cycle of the worm and then proceeded to a reeling room where silk was reeled from seven cocoons simultaneously by hand. Each cocoon yields two miles of silk. This very interesting outing finished in a shop, where we were able to make purchases.

APPENDIX 5

Porter v Bond 1873

A summary of the thirteen-page legal document in End Note 21, the family background and implications for the Bonds

Evidence shows that Barnabas Mayston's father, Barnabas Bond the elder, born 1801[318] had been a co-executor of the 1856 will of one Mary Porter's brother, Rev. John Mills. The public records show that Rev. John Mills' significant will of "effects under £25,000"[319] was proved[320] at Bury St Edmunds on 23 January 1861 by a cited Barnabas Bond of Alburgh, who was described as "Gentleman the surviving Executor".[321]

This is indeed Barnabas Bond the elder, the father of Barnabas Mayston, and on Rev. Mills' death in 1860 he had found himself as the only living executor, since co-executor Edward Mills had predeceased Rev. John Mills (Edward's brother), and all but one other legatee had also died in the meantime.

The one surviving legatee was the afore-mentioned Rev. John Mills' sister Mary Porter (née Mills), the plaintiff in this case. She had reportedly lived beyond what was then deemed to be the 'child-bearing age', without having borne any children to whom her brother's estate might have been transferable. Furthermore, at this time before the first legislation on the matter,[322] Mary Porter's capacity, being a married woman, to inherit actual property was legally constrained: she was entitled to receive only the monetary income derived from her brother Rev. John Mills' stocks and shares and not the real estate. Disastrously for her, those financial investments had collapsed in value. Her plea therefore was that the property assets of her brother's estate should be converted into accessible cash.

Barnabas Bond the elder, as executor, was in overall possession of the property assets for distribution according to the will. They comprised significant copyhold and other properties. He had placed them on mortgage for the future benefit of his own son and only heir-at-law our Barnabas Mayston Bond. But then, in 1873, he too had died. Infelicitously, his own will did not specifically provide for a contingency whereby any estate for which he was a trustee or mortgagee could be passed smoothly to his heirs. The record shows Rebecca Ann his widow proved his will of "effects under £6,000"[323] at Norwich on 20th February 1873.

In view of the above-mentioned (up to) £25,000 in legacy from Rev. John Mills back in 1861 it seems that a residual amount of the legacy was trapped in non-liquid capital. Rebecca Ann also was not only legally incapable of inheriting her late husband Barnabas the elder's inherited property. She was also powerless to convert the residual stocks and shares into monetary funds that could have provided Mary Porter (née Mills) with the income due to her - even if Rebecca Ann had had the intention of doing so. Hence the recourse to law by both parties, it would seem.

"Barnabas Bond of Norfolk" is recorded in the England and Wales Marriage Registers as having wed a Martha Mills in 1828. This was indeed Barnabas the elder's first marriage, and although not conclusively evidenced, it is pretty certain that this wife Martha was the sister of Rev. John Mills. She was also the sister of Edward Mills, and of Mary Porter (née Mills) the latter who was plaintiff in this *Porter v Bond* 1873 case. If you have kept up with this so far, you will now have worked out that Barnabas the elder was, via his first wife Martha, a past brother-in-law of Rev. John Mills.

A sad story surrounds Barnabas the elder's first family. At the ages of 35 and 30 respectively, he and Martha were noted as living at Alburgh.[324] Sadly, their daughter Anna died in 1844 and their son Barnabas Frederick died in May 1846, both aged 14. Martha herself had died in January 1846, aged 39. Sometime after the deaths of Martha and both of his children, actually in 1859, the widower Barnabas the elder then married a second wife, Rebecca Ann from which union came the birth of Barnabas Mayston, our future doctor of Leyton, in 1861[325] as briefly recorded in Chapter One.

There are numerous mentions in nineteenth-century electoral lists of the property ownership statuses of Barnabas Bond (the elder) both in Alburgh and in another Norfolk village: Pulham St Mary the Virgin. Barnabas Mayston Bond, his son, was to retain titles to properties there until 1919 even though he was not resident. The assumption must be that the judge at Chancery in 1873 upheld Barnabas the elder's will and enabled property titles to pass to his son Barnabas Mayston perhaps on the coming of age. The particular relevance for our story is that details of Barnabas Mayston (the future Dr Bond)'s location and professional circumstances year-by-year are revealed to us via these annual records of the parish Out Voters of the time.

The court in the *Porter v Bond* 1873 case had the task of determining the legally-inheritable proportions of the Rev John Mills' legacy between his surviving sister Mary Porter, and his late brother-in-law's widow Rebecca Ann. Whatever the outcome for the Porters, it would seem that sufficient funds remained with the Bonds for Rebecca Ann to spend her widowhood in central London, then retire to Bromley Kent and for Barnabas Mayston to have been put through University Hospital Medical School, from where in 1886 he qualified both as a Member of the Royal College of Surgeons of England and as a Licentiate of the Royal College of Physicians of London.[326]

End Notes

1. Vintage bromide print, 1952, by John Gay. Note spelling 'Zoe'. ©National Portrait Gallery image 126630.
2. *So Spins the Silkworm*, Zoë Lady Hart Dyke, Rockliff, London 1949, later in the text referred to as *So Spins the Silkworm*.
3. John Martin, *Oxford Dictionary of National Biography* September 2004. Later referred to as *Oxford Biography*.
4. See www.moruslondinium.org for research project on London's mulberries.
5. *So Spins the Silkworm* page 142.
6. Ellen Buxton, the second daughter of the Buxton family resident at Leytonstone House, recorded details in writing and drawing of her childhood life. This one shows the mulberry tree at Leytonstone House providing enjoyment for the children. See *Family Sketchbook – A Hundred Years Ago,* by E. Ellen Buxton. Fig. 3 shows the actual tree still standing in Leytonstone today, 140 years later.
7. en.wikipedia.org/wiki/List_of_extant_baronetcies#Baronetage_of_England. The Dyke family originated at Dykesfield, Cumberland, before the Norman Conquest and branches later settled at Henfield in Sussex and at Cranbrook in Kent. Reginald de Dike of Cranbrook was Sheriff of Kent in 1355. Thomas Dyke (d.1632) of Cranbrook married Joan Walsh, heiress of the manor of Horeham in the parish of Waldron in Sussex, which thus passed to the Dykes. The Dyke Baronetcy, of Horeham in the County of Sussex, is title no. 116 in the Baronetage of England.
8. *An Englishman's Home. The Adventures of an Eccentric Gardener*, Tom Hart Dyke, Bantam Press, London 2007, page 134. Later referred to as *An Englishman's Home*
9. As reproduced in *British History Online,* originally published by Victoria County History, London, 1973, later referred to as *A History of the County of Essex: Volume 6.*
10. *A History of the County of Essex: Volume 6.*
11. Evidenced in Birth Place and Employment columns of the 1901 and 1911 censuses.
12. Both entries from UK Medical Registers 1859 – 1959.
13. Incidentally, not far from Lullingstone Castle in Eynsford, Kent, where Millicent Zoë, Rebecca Ann's granddaughter, would later reside.
14. National Probate Calendar Index of Wills and Administration.
15. According to www.moneysorter.co.uk/calculator_inflation2.html the equivalent sum in 2017 would be £360,918.
16. *A History of the County of Essex: Volume 6.*
17. "an exclusive residential street and had gates at either end to restrict entry" https://en.wikipedia.org/wiki/Doughty_Street.
18. 1881 census.
19. England and Wales National Probate Calendar Index of Wills and Administration.
20. According to www.moneysorter.co.uk/calculator_inflation2.html - the equivalent sum in 2017 would be £474,360.
21. Cause Number 1873 P35 *Porter v Bond*: The National Archives (TNA) C16/884/P35. (see Fig. 4 and Appendix 5).
22. Fig. 5: Alburgh Church contemporary photograph courtesy of Sophie Yeomans of Norwich, 2015.
23. Francis White's *History, Gazetteer and Directory of Norfolk,* 1854 pages 376 – 377.
24. Derived from Norfolk Church of England Baptism records, Diss, 1773 and contextual genealogical data.

25. 1861 census at "Gentleman's House" in Alburgh with three servants and employing 33 men and 13 boys.
26. 1871 census at "Cherry Tree" Alburgh farming 556 acres with 25 labourers.
27. Marriage certificate and banns issued from St James Clerkenwell, possibly the parish appropriate for Barnabas's university lodgings.
28. Treyarnon. A current attraction of nearby St Merryn is the Rick Stein pub restaurant The Cornish Arms.
29. 1861 census.
30. London, England, Non-Conformist Registers 1694 – 1921: George Ernest Luxon of Aldersgate Street London, baptised at Jewry Street Methodist Chapel in London 12 June 1864.
31. London, England, Church of England Marriages and Banns 1754 – 1921.
32. Ordnance Survey London 23 SW 1912 – 1914, courtesy of Waltham Forest Archives, Vestry House, London E17.
33. *So Spins the Silkworm* page 1.
34. Tremain was the maiden name of Walter's grandmother, Eliza Luxon.
35. Restored in 1945 following a fire.
36. As yet un-researched.
37. Reproduced with permission of www.history-in-pictures.co.uk/store/images/uploads/Images%20550/Images/E/E-0539.jpg.
38. *A History of the Parish of Leyton, Essex*. John Kennedy, Phelp Brothers, Leyton, 1894. Page 67 records a plain cruciform building of stone.
39. Note that the All Saints Church, now still standing, was built in 1973 when the Beaumont Estate was being constructed by Waltham Forest Council.
40. https://ukga.org/england/Essex/towns/Leyton.html
41. Walthamstow Parish Register, St Saviour's Church 1886 – 1892 accessed at Waltham Forest Archives, Vestry House, London E17.
42. Death certificate of Hugh Trevor Bond.
43. en.wikipedia.org/wiki/Tracheotomy; en.wikipedia.org/wiki/Diphtheria.
44. 1901 census: Dr Peskett's house located between Barclay House and Chingford Hall where he lived with his family.
45. UK Medical Registers 1908: Dr Peskett's address recorded as Leyton Town Hall.
46. UK Medical Registers 1895.
47. Wellcome Library SA/SMO online retrieved 15 August 2015.
48. Date and source of photograph unknown.
49. *British Medical Journal*, 25 August 1900 page 511.
50. ezitis.myzen.co.uk/eastern.html.
51. (UK Medical Registers 1859 – 1959). 1896 records Millicent Zoë's birth at Leyton, but by 1899 Dr Bond's medical registration is at Poole.
52. *So Spins the Silkworm* page 1.
53. Norfolk Register of Electors, Southern Division, Pulham Market District, Parish of Pulham St Mary the Virgin.
54. Copyholding was a mediaeval form of property tenure that survived in English law until 1925.
55. National Probate Calendar Index of Wills and Administration records Eliza Luxon's 1913 address as 30 Brook Green, Hammersmith, with probate going to her daughter Eliza Josephine Bond wife of Barnabas Mayston Bond.
56. *The Medical Register* for 1899 (the previous one was 1895) gives Dr Bond's address as 100 High Street, Poole, Dorset. 1903 states Westwood (Poole). Registers from 1907 – 1919 give 30

End Notes

Brook Green, Hammersmit,h London W6.
57. *So Spins the Silkworm* pages 3, 4.
58. From 1965 for 50 years this amalgamated building was the Austrian Catholic Centre hostel, Charity Commission No. 240816.
59. Lane's Masonic Records, version 1.0 (<http://www.hrionline.ac.uk/lane>, October 2011). HRI Online Pubns, ISBN 978-0-955-7876-8-3.
60. Norfolk Registers of Electors, 1897 annually to 1911: Southern Division of Norfolk.
61. *The Medical Register* 1935.
62. *Keynes on Population*, John Toye, Oxford, 2000.
63. It was in this part of Devon that Barnabas Mayston, her brother would much later spend his last years.
64. 1901 census: at Mary C. Richardson's boarding house 17 Powis Lane, North Kensington.
65. 1891 census: at the residence of musician Frederick Crowe and his wife in Upton, Torquay.
66. A younger brother had died in infancy in 1863.
67. National Probate Calendar Index of Wills and Administration.
68. According to www.ukmoneysorter.co.uk the equivalent sum in 2017 would be £103,114.
69. 1918 Electoral Register for Hammersmith & Fulham.
70. British Army WW1 Medal Rolls Index Cards 1914 – 1920.
71. *So Spins the Silkworm* page 1.
72. Note that 'silkworms' are not worms but are caterpillars that spin cocoons around themselves at their chrysalis stage.
73. *So Spins the Silkworm* page 3.
74. *So Spins the Silkworm* page 3.
75. *An Englishman's Home* page 121. See Appendix 2A for detail of Tom Hart Dyke's grandson relationship to Zoë.
76. (1826 – 1913) an unconventional writer, hostess, horticulturist and plant collector connected to the British establishment who bred silkworms: en.wikipedia.org/wiki/ Lady Dorothy Nevill.
77. (1871 – 1919) a German philosopher, political activist, linguist, painter and botanist who identified and preserved plant specimens. She pressed this mulberry ('morus alba') sprig in June 1913 at Berlin prison. See *Herbarium* Rosa Luxemburg, Dietz, Berlin 2010, plate 153.
78. See discussion in *Virginia Woolf and the Study of Nature*, Christine Alt, Cambridge University Press, 2010, page 80.
79. *Silk Fit for a Prince*, Godfrey Winn, article page 28 in *Woman* magazine 5th July 1969.
80. By this time Walter Tremayne would have been away at boarding school.
81. By Robert Galbraith (aka J K Rowling), Mulholland Books 2014.
82. Jake Kerridge in *The Telegraph*, 11 June 2014.
83. *So Spins the Silkworm* page 36. Zoë's first experiment at stifling was in the kitchen oven: "on cutting open a cocoon and examining the chrysalis I found that it was bone dry and quite dead".
84. See copy of letter to author, addressed to 9 Manor Road, at Appendix 3C.
85. St Paul's Girls' School opened in 1904; the original St Paul's School had been founded for boys in the sixteenth century: http://spgs.org/.
86. As pictured in Fig. 10.
87. His first name of Walter was dropped at some point in favour of his middle name 'Tremayne'.
88. *So Spins the Silkworm* page 8.
89. Alumnae http://spgs.org/. Later Old Paulinas included Marghanita Laski, Monica Dickens (expelled) and [Dame] Celia Johnson. Contemporary Old Paulinas: Imogen Stubbs, Rachel

Weisz, Shirley Williams, Harriet Harman: en.wikipedia.org/wiki/St Paul's Girls' School.
90. http://saumur-jadis.pagesperso-orange.fr/recit/ch40/r40d6fil.htm. This website records the history of Saumur and includes *Saumur-Jadis: Étude encyclopédique sur l'histoire de Saumur à partir de quatre entrée'*, by Joseph-Henri Denécheau, in which the *Collège des Jeunes Filles* is featured in detail. Photographs in Fig. 13 and Fig. 14 are reproduced by kind permission of M. Denécheau.
91. *So Spins the Silkworm* pages 10 – 12 describe Zoë climbing out of an upper window at night to retrieve silkworm eggs from this dubious accomplice.
92. www.zpag.net/Noeuds/cravate/cravate.htm.
93. *So Spins the Silkworm* pages 8 – 9.
94. *So Spins the Silkworm* page 14.
95. *So Spins the Silkworm* page 15.
96. *So Spins the Silkworm* page 17.
97. *So Spins the Silkworm* page 17.
98. *So Spins the Silkworm* page 17.
99. *So Spins the Silkworm* page 15.
100. *So Spins the Silkworm* page 19.
101. Later expounded by his son Oliver Guy Hart Dyke in *Lullingstone Castle and The World Garden*, Tony Russell Associates 2008, page 2.
102. This High Anglican fashionable society church was rebuilt at Kingsbury, Middlesex in 1933 – 34, see blogs.ucl.ac.uk/survey-of-london/2016/04/01/st-andrews-church/ and www.brent.gov.uk/media/3023983/Kingsburys%20Recycled%20Church.pdf.
103. Likely to have been Oliver Augustus' cousin Robert Percyvall Hart Dyke: see http://www.thepeerage.com/p31956.htm#i319551.
104. Marriage certificate. Banns are the public reading in church on three Sundays prior to a wedding, giving the chance for anyone to raise an objection. Clearly, no-one had.
105. *Kent & Sussex Courier*, 4 August 1922, copyright Local World Limited courtesy of The British Library via Genes Reunited International copyright Brightsolid Online Publishing 2014. Also in the *Folkestone, Hythe, Sandgate & Cheriton Herald* on 5 August 1922.
106. See End Note 102.
107. Marriage certificate.
108. City of London Royal Fusiliers 1915 – 1916, British Army WW1 Medal Rolls.
109. Marriage certificate.
110. https://en.wikipedia.org/wiki/Dyke_baronets.
111. Tom remarks in *An Englishman's Home* page 138 "So when it comes to class, I have no idea which one I am in and I couldn't care less. I do find it quite funny that one day I might end up *Sir* Thomas Hart Dyke the 11th baronet, because the 10th baronet my cousin David in Toronto, Uncle Derek's son, has no kids." Oliver and Sarah's daughter Anya (born 1978), Tom's sister, is not in line at all, due to the inheritance gender restrictions mentioned elsewhere in this book.
112. www.lullingstonecastle.co.uk/the-world-garden-grounds/.
113. www.independent.co.uk/news/people/profiles/passedfailed-an-education-in-the-life-of-tom-hart-dyke-orchid-hunter-6103275.html.
114. *So Spins the Silkworm* page 48.
115. www.thepeerage.com/p17638.htm#i176375, www.william1.co.uk/w191.htm.
116. Since renamed and now known as *Beeches*, Tyrells Wood. Surrey Industrial History Group Newsletter, 16 July 2008.
117. *So Spins the Silkworm* page 19.
118. *So Spins the Silkworm* page 19.
119. *So Spins the Silkworm* page 34.

End Notes

120. *Oxford Biography.*
121. *So Spins the Silkworm* page 118.
122. *So Spins the Silkworm* page 34.
123. *So Spins the Silkworm* page 51.
124. *So Spins the Silkworm* page 52.
125. *So Spins the Silkworm* page 55.
126. 15th September 2017
127. http://thepeerage.com/p31956.htm#i319551.
128. *So Spins the Silkworm* page 48.
129. 'The Rt. Hon. Sir William Hart Dyke Bart.', Fred Whyler, in *Journal of North West Kent Family History Society,* vol 7, no. 9, page 317. Later information records that the brewery sold the land on to Kent County Council.
130. *Lullingstone Castle and the World Garden.* Tony Russell Associates, 2008, page 2.
131. *Lullingstone Castle and The World Garden* Tony Russell Associates, 2008, page 2.
132. www.britishpathe.com/video/silkworms-receive-blessing/query/Lullingstone. See *Selected Bibliography and References* later.
133. *So Spins the Silkworm* pages 20 – 33.
134. *So Spins the Silkworm* page 32.
135 *So Spins the Silkworm* page 67.
136. *Oxford Biography.*
137. Although the visit of Queen Mary was a private one, the Kent local press reported it with an article (see text in *Selected Bibliography and References 3*) and a photograph (not shown): http://www.kenthistoryforum.co.uk/index.php?topic=11393.0. Posted by KYN on 3 June 2012. The photograph on that website is unattributed and could have been taken by local photographer John Topham. The very similar photograph here, at Fig. 17 is by John Topham, whose photographic archive is held at Topfoto Ltd.
138. Queen Mary of Teck, dressed in black, had been widowed six months earlier, on the death of King George V 20 January 1936.
139. *So Spins the Silkworm* page 63.
140. This scene has reportedly been depicted in one of four unattributed unpublished and currently unavailable humorous sketches issued on 17 February 1948. One of the images portrays an additional scene of the royal visit, a third drawing appears to show the presentation of an award, and the fourth image is of a silkworm attached to a mulberry leaf.
141. Betty Joel (1894 – 1985) Ray Foulk in *Furniture and Cabinet Making,* 31 August 2011.
142. Date of *Coronation Exhibition* unknown, but the actual coronation took place on 11 December 1936.
143. https://en.wikipedia.org/wiki/Betty_Joel.
144. *So Spins the Silkworm* page 73.
145. *Oxford Biography.*
146. *So Spins the Silkworm* page 115.
147. en.wikipedia.org/wiki/Warner_%26_Son.
148. *Weaving and the Warners 1870 – 1970,* Sir Ernest Goodale, F. Lewis Publishers Ltd, Leigh-on-Sea, 1971, page 47.
149. *So Spins the Silkworm* page 67 – 68.
150. *Journal of the Royal Society of Arts* 25 December 1936, pages 152 – 165.
151. *The Lullingstone Silk Farm,* Lady Hart Dyke. Lecture at Fourth Ordinary Meeting of Royal Society for the Encouragement of Arts, Manufactures and Commerce, 25 November 1936. *Journal of the RSA* 25 December 1936, page 159. *Selected Bibliography and References 2.*
152. *So Spins the Silkworm* page 61.
153. *So Spins the Silkworm* page 68.

154. *The Telegraph* 24 April 2011: 'Royal weddings past from 1795 to 1981'.
155. On Sunday 30 July 2017, at Lullingstone Castle.
156. *An Englishman's Home* page 125
157. *The Gravesend Reporter* 5 January 2011. See additional quotation in *Selected Bibliography and References 3*.
158. *An Englishman's Home* page 119.
159. 'Under the Counter' Noel Whitcomb. Undated and unattributed news-cutting likely from the *Daily Mirror* 1947 (when Whitcomb's journalist career began) up to 1956 (after which the silk farm was no longer at Lullingstone). Whitcomb's obituary in *The Independent* August 1993.
160. Whitcomb reports Zoë saying her daughter was a Young Cochran girl. This was a high-stepping dance team famed in West End revues.
161. *An Englishman's Home* page 135.
162. *So Spins the Silkworm* page 51.
163. www.smith.edu/hsc/silk/papers/baird.html.
164. *Journal of the Royal Society of Arts* December 25th 1936, page 158.
165. *So Spins the Silkworm* page 84.
166. *So Spins the Silkworm* page xi.
167. *Biological Diversity: Exploiters and Exploited,* Paul E. Hatcher, Nick Battey; Wiley-Blackwell 2011. However note that this source states that Zoë "kept silkworms as a child at Lullingstone" which, disappointingly, is factually incorrect.
168. *Surrey Mirror* 17 June 1949 accessed via *The British Newspaper Archive* July 2015.
169. *The London Gazette* 1 March 1949 page 1069.
170. *So Spins the Silkworm* page 138.
171. Accessed from The National Archives (TNA) September 2017.
172. File D1054, Document 5.
173. ARC File A 1157 (not further identified and not released by TNA).
174. Minute of 26 January 1954.
175. File D1054, Document 3.
176. Dated 5 February 1954.
177. Document 2, File D1054.
178. *Yes Minister* www.bbc.co.uk/comedy/yesminister/.
179. *An Englishman's Home* page 133.
180. *Paulina* March 1940, St Paul's Girls School, courtesy Howard Bailes.
181. *So Spins the Silkworm* page 89.
182. *So Spins the Silkworm* page 107.
183. *So Spins the Silkworm* page 101.
184. Likely to have been Royal Army Medical Corps.
185. *So Spins the Silkworm* page 124-5.
186. *Hartlepool Mail, Durham,* 7 February 1944, July 2015.
187. This wording in the Hartlepool Mail is expressed in the legal reported-speech convention of the day, which comes over now as unclear.
188. UK Outward Passenger Lists and Inward Passenger Lists 1930, Nelson Line.
189. Grace's Guide to British Industrial History details his stand at the British Industries Fair *www.gracesguide.co.uk/Lullingstone_Silk_Farm.*
190. *Oxford Biography.*
191. *So Spins the Silkworm* page 132.
192. *So Spins the Silkworm* page 132.
193. 'With 1948 comes the Silver Jubilee of the Daily Mail Ideal Home Exhibition', Margaret Sherman, *Daily Mail Ideal Home Book 1947 – 48, Daily Mail* Exhibition Department

End Notes

194. For example major museums and collections including: metmuseum.org/art/collection/search/119421; http://www.meg-andrews.com/item-details/Arnold-Lever/6594; http://collections.vam.ac.uk/item/O72683/london-wall-head-scarf-lever-arnold/; https://collection.sciencemuseum.org.uk/people/cp121045/arnold-lever; http://scarfcollectoruk.co.uk/page%201.html; https://www.rennart.co.uk/website.pdfs/londonsquares.pdf; http://alfiesantiques.blogspot.co.uk/2012/12/vintage-scarves-by-arnold-lever.html.
195. *So Spins the Silkworm* page 134.
196. https://www.pinterest.co.uk/ahyatt345/my-vintage-scarves/.
197. www.liveauctioneers.com/item/5018845_2096-a-jacqmar-printed-silk-ballet-design-headscarf-1#&gid=1&pid=2.
198. Kerry Taylor, London SE1.
199. *Lullingstone Silk Farm 1932 – 1955*, Zoe Lady Hart Dyke, Dimond & Co Ltd, Dartford, Kent, page 70.
200. *Industrial Archaeology of Hertfordshire*, W. Branch Johnson, David & Charles, Newton Abbott 1970, as quoted in www.hertfordshire-genealogy.co.uk/data/occupations/silk.htm: silk mills at Baldock, Hatfield, Hitchin, Redbourn, Rickmansworth, St Albans, Tring, Watford.
201. https://historicengland.org.uk/listing/the-list/list-entry/1348110.
202. https://www.nationaltrust.org.uk/shaws-corner.
203. Lullingstone Silk Farm 1957 visitor brochure centre page (not illustrated in *Select Bibliography and References*).
204. *Lullingstone Silk Farm 1932 – 1955*, Zoë Lady Hart Dyke, Dimond & Co. Ltd, Dartford, Kent, page 9.
205. https://collection.nam/ac/uk/inventory/objects/results/1994-05-419: Page 23 : kitbag 1939 – 46 owned by Major Ronald Field Bibb Royal Engineers Wessex TA.
206. *So Spins the Silkworm* page xi.
207. *So Spins the Silkworm* page 99.
208. *So Spins the Silkworm* page 97.
209. Photograph by John Topham (topfoto.co.uk) originally published in 'Silkworms in England Spin for the Queen', John E. H. Nolan, *National Geographic,* 1953 page 689. See *Selected Bibliography and References 2.* Behind Zoe is the banner of the Women's Farm and Garden Association (WFGA), a forerunner of the Land Army movement and founded in 1899.
210. Marriage certificate.
211. General Records Office Index of Births.
212. Birth certificate.
213. Massachusetts Passenger & Crew Lists.
214. New York Passenger Lists.
215. *Lullingstone Silk Farm 1932 – 1955*, Zoë Lady Hart Dyke, Dimond & Co Ltd, Dartford, Kent, page 19.
216. Death certificate of Ronald Field Bibb.
217. Death certificate of Vera Doris Kate Ellis (née Mead).
218. *Weaving and the Warners 1870 – 1970*, Sir Ernest Goodale, F. Lewis Publishers Ltd, Leigh-on-Sea 1971.
219. 'A Sale as Smooth as Silk', Sarah Edghill, in *The Telegraph,* 20 March 2004.
220. www.gracesguide.co.uk/Lullingstone_Silk_Farm.
221. *Wedding Babylon: Confessions of a Wedding Planner,* Imogen Edwards-Jones, Random, 2011.
222. *So Spins the Silkworm*, page xi.
223. As Honorary Secretary of the Huntingdonshire County Council. Supplement to *London Gazette* 7 June 1918.
224. en.wikipedia.org/wiki/Lina_Scott_Gatty.
225. www.revolvy.com/main/index.php?s=Lina Scott Gatty. Published in the UK on 28 January

1922, 28 October 1922 and 30 October 1922. en.wikipedia.org/wiki/Lina_Scott_Gatty. creativecommons.org/licenses/by-sa/3.0/.
226. http://www.thepeerage.com/p33071.htm.
227. Marriage certificate.
228. Alexander John Scott Gatty had remarried in 1927: GRO Indices of Marriages.
229. en.wikipedia.org/wiki/Augustus_Duncombe.
230. 14 Manor House Marylebone Road, London NW1.
231. 20 Devonshire Place, London W1.
232. Data in this paragraph are sourced variously from England & Wales Civil Registration Births and Deaths Indices, London England Electoral Registers 1832 – 1965, British Phone Books 1880 – 1984 and England & Wales National Probate Calendar.
233. *Daily Mercury*, Mackay, Queensland, Australia, 15 October 1947.
234. *So Spins the Silkworm* page 85.
235. Extract from undated photograph copyright samuelryder.net. http://samuelryder.net/gallery/ (since closed). Photograph reproduced by kind permission of Mr Tom Ryder.
236. International golfing tournament described within the Ryder family website samuelryder.net (since closed).
237. *So Spins the Silkworm* page 86.
238. Heath and Heather Ltd was later to become the health food shop company 'Holland & Barratt'.
239. *So Spins the Silkworm* page 113.
240. Eleanour Sophy Sinclair Rohde (1881 – 1950) gardener, horticultural writer of note, whose work at Lullingstone Castle was one of her most visited designs: en.wikipedia.org/wiki/Eleanour_Sinclair_Rohde.
241. Oliver Guy Hart Dyke, 30 July 2017.
242. *So Spins the Silkworm* page 113.
243. *The Author's and Writer's Who's Who*. Sixth edition. Darien, CT: Hafner Publishing Co., 1971. (Au&Wr) *The International Authors and Writers Who's Who*. Seventh edition. Edited by Ernest Kay. Cambridge, England: International Biographical Centre, 1976. (IntAu&W 7).
244. *So Spins the Silkworm* page 77. Mary Benedetta would also interview the young Alfred Hitchcock ('Alfred Hitchcock Interviews' in *The Star*, Sidney Gottlieb, 14 July 1938) who had been born in nearby Leytonstone in 1899.
245. *Street Markets of London*, Mary Benedetta, photography L Moholy-Nagy, 1936, John Miles Ltd. Reissued B. Blom, New York, 1972.
246. *So Spins the Silkworm* page 135.
247. Image of Mrs Henderson reproduced here from www.theroses.co.uk. Courtesy of David Rose.
248. https://en.wikipedia.org/wiki/Laura_Henderson accessed 17 August 2015. See also https://en.wikipedia.org/wiki/Mrs_Henderson_Presents
249. http://www.independent.co.uk/arts-entertainment/films/news/sex-censorship-and-the-real-mrs-henderson-514952.html.
250. *So Spins the Silkworm* page 98.
251. https://www.architectsjournal.co.uk/comment/who-designed-the-1938-empire-exhibition-womens-pavilion/8642299. 17 August 2015.
252. Publication licence for this image purchased from *Historic Environment Scotland*.
253. Lady Elgin: Katherine Elizabeth Bruce, DBE, the wife of 10th Earl of Elgin & 14th Earl of Kincardine.
254. *So Spins the Silkworm* page 79.
255. Artificially advance the leaf maturation to stimulate the silk-worm feeding process in out-of-season May.

End Notes

256. Christopher Lee, *The Independent*, 22 April 1997.
257. http://www.independent.co.uk/news/people/obituary-margaret-brodie-1268627.html accessed 17 August 2015.
258. *So Spins the Silkworm* page 15.
259. According to www.ukmoneysorter.co.uk the equivalent sum in 2017 would be £20,491.
260. England & Wales National Probate Calendar.
261. England and Wales National Probate Calendar.
262. Parish, GRO and other records accessed 2015 – 2016.
263. Accessed 2015, 2016.
264. According to www.moneysorter.co.uk/calculator_inflation2.html the equivalent sum in 2017 would be £114,037.
265. Australia Marriage Index 1788 – 1950 page 794 vol 322.
266. *So Spins the Silkworm* page 17.
267. UK Outward Passenger Lists 1890 – 1960 accessed 2015.
268. GRO National Records, Kew.
269. Medical Practitioners lists in the *South Australia Police Gazette* for each of those years.
270. *South Australian Police Gazette* 14 November 1923, page 310.
271. UK Incoming Passenger Lists.
272. *So Spins the Silkworm* page 17.
273. *London Gazette* Supplement 28 September 1945.
274. Post Office Directory, 1938.
275. UK Outgoing Passenger Lists.
276. British Army WW1 Medal Rolls Index Cards 1914 – 20; UK WW1 Service Medals and Award Rolls 1914 – 1920.
277. Lane's Masonic Records, version 1.0 (http://www.hrionline.ac.uk/lane, October 2011). HRI Online Pubns, ISBN 978-0-955-7876-8-3.
278. Email to author from website support 21 May 2017.
279. UK Outgoing Passenger Lists.
280. www.bsbb.org.uk/content/pages/documents/1449249883.pdf.
281. Obituary in BMJ journal 3 September 1988.
282. At Barons Court, W14.
283. England & Wales Probate Calendar.
284. According to www.ukmoneysorter.co.uk the equivalent sum in 2017 would be £19,232.
285. *The Advertiser*, Adelaide, Tuesday 27 November 1934. http://nla.gov.au/nla.news-article35021501.
286. Death Index Caroline Annie Bond born 14 August 1886, died Hove, 1973 4th Quarter. National Wills & Probate: Caroline Annie Bond at Brighton 12 November 1973 leaving £1,770.
287. UK Passenger lists accessed March 2017, unaccompanied by a spouse and leaving from a Devon address.
288. UK Passenger lists accessed March 2017, unaccompanied by a spouse and destination address of 41 Glyn Road, Clapton, London.
289. England & Wales National Probate Calendar 1973 – 1995.
290. According www.moneysorter.co.uk/calculator_inflation2.html the equivalent sum in 2017 would be £15,777.
291. *So Spins the Silkworm* page 87.
292. *An Englishman's Home* page 134.
293. *So Spins the Silkworm* page 1
294. *So Spins the Silkworm* page 139.
295. *Daily Mercury*, Mackay, Queensland, Australia, 15 October 1947.

296. Mentioned in *So Spins the Silkworm*, but so far uncorroborated with any public records.
297. For instance there is no mention in http://www.bbc.co.uk/radio4/womanshour/timeline/1930.shtml.
298. Parity of esteem between academic and vocational education and training in Britain: see for example http://www.spicker.uk/social-policy/education.htm for a contemporary summary of research in this area: Paul Spicker *Education and Social Policy, an introduction to social policy*, accessed 15 January 2018.
299. *An Englishman's Home* page 133.
300. *Oxford Biography*.
301. *The New Sylva: A Discourse on Forest and Orchard Trees for the Twenty-first Century*, Gabriel Hemery and Sarah Simblet, Bloomsbury, London, 2014, page 186.
302. www.moruslondinium.org/research/mulberries-and-silk-john-feltwell accessed November 2016.
303. *Lullingstone Castle and the World Garden*, Russell 2008, page 19, page 28.
304. www.kenthistoryforum.co.uk/index.php?topic=11393. Eynsford, Kent.
305. Succession to the Crown Act 2013.
306. Lord Trefgarne's Private Members' Equality (Titles) Bill ran out of Parliamentary time in 2016.
307. Some general information in these paragraphs is compiled from data at en.wikipedia.org/wiki/Baronet.
308. The second wife of her ex-husband Sir Oliver Augustus Hamilton 8th Baronet, and the wife of her son Sir Derek William 9th Baronet.
309. *Kelly's Directory* 1890 Essex Leyton.
310. *The Grange, with Emphasis on the Lane Family*, David Ian Chapman, Leyton & Leytonstone Historical Society, 2007.
311. Albeit his service was 1616 to 1619 and he would not have been the scribe in 1609 en.wikipedia.org/wiki/Secretary_of_State_(England).
312. See *The Grange* page 7.
313. In *History of Leyton vol 1*, Bren Kennedy, accessed at Waltham Forest Archives, Vestry House Museum, London E17.
314. www.gardeningknowhow.com/ornamental/trees/fruitless-mulberry/fruitless-mulberry-trees.htm.
315. www.moruslondinium.org/map accessed November 2016.
316. www.newham.gov.uk/Documents/Environment and planning/StratfordStJohnsConservationAreaAppraisalFINAL[1].pdf, pages 34 – 35.
317. From http://mulberrytrees.co.uk/locations/ http://en.wikipedia.org/wiki/Stratford_London accessed 25 August 2015.
318. Norfolk Church of England Baptism records for Billingford and Thorpe Parva.
319. According to http://www.moneysorter.co.uk/calculator_inflation2.html the equivalent sum in 2017 would be £2,080,526.
320. Note that the probate appoints the executor as having legal power to dispose of a testator's assets in accordance with the will.
321. National Probate Calendar Index of Wills and Administration.
322. en.wikipedia.org/wiki/Married_Women's_Property_Act_1870.
323. England and Wales National Probate Calendar Index of Wills 1873.
324. 1841 census.
325. Deaths, marriage and birth in this paragraph listed in pertinent England & Wales Indexes, accessed 2016 – 17.
326. UK Medical Registers 1859 – 1959.

ALPHABETICAL INDEX

Alburgh 11, 12, 13, 85, 111, 112
Alexander Scott Gatty 71
Amanda Farr 41, 123
Anna Zinkeisen 49
Anya Hart Dyke 53
Arnold Lever 64
Association of Women Executives 90
Australia 81, 82, 85, 86, 90
Ayot St Lawrence 7, 67
Barnabas Bond the elder 12, 24, 111
Barnabas Mayston Bond 7, 8, 11, 12, 13, 14, 17, 20, 23, 37, 41, 79, 80, 81, 82, 85, 111, 112
baronetcy 8, 35, 36, 37, 43
Basil Tremayne 84
BBC 47, 74
Betty Joel Galleries 49
Bibb 67, 88
Board of Trade 60
Bond 7, 8, 10, 11, 12, 13, 14, 15, 17, 18, 19, 20, 21, 22, 23, 24, 25, 26, 28, 30, 34, 35, 36, 37, 38, 42, 79, 80, 81, 82, 83, 84, 85, 86, 107, 111, 112
Boston Museum of Fine Arts 64
Brook Green 22, 24, 25, 30, 38, 80
business 46, 55, 57, 62, 65, 73, 77, 87, 88
Cambridge 12, 13, 20, 21, 23
Captain Antonio Crivellari 71
Captain David Hart Dyke 41
Capworth Street 11, 18
Caroline Annie 80, 81, 82, 85, 86, 121
Caroline Annie Woods 80, 81, 82, 85
Cecil G. Marston 35, 36
China 52, 56
class 10, 11, 26, 31, 32, 46, 71, 78, 83, 84, 88
cocoons 26, 42, 46, 52, 55, 67, 90
Collège des Jeunes Filles 31, 32, 44
Colonel Field Bibb 57
Cornwall 11, 14, 15, 79, 84
Dame Laura Knight 49
David and Elizabeth Emmanuel 69
David Gansel 107
David Ian Chapman 107

Denécheau 31, 32
Derek Hart Dyke 39
Devon 23, 24, 80, 83, 85
Diane Josephine 84
divorce 8, 62, 85, 103
Dorset 16, 21, 26, 30, 69
Dr Peskett 19
eccentricity 43, 71, 77, 78, 88
economics 53, 54, 55
education 23, 26, 31, 35
Egypt 25, 43, 82, 83, 85
Eileen Hunter 49
Eleanor Sinclair Rohde 73
Eliza Bond 7, 15
Eliza Josephine 11, 14, 17, 24, 25, 28, 32, 34, 37, 38, 79, 81, 82, 83, 84, 85
Elsie Margaret 17, 25, 26, 37, 38, 54, 79, 83, 84, 85
Empire Exhibition 77
engineer 35, 38, 53, 82
Ernest Goodale 50
Essex 7, 11, 12, 15, 21
Evelyn May Hardy 38, 83
Eynsford 43
female 23, 75, 77
féministes 32
feminists 33
First World War 8, 24, 33, 38, 85
France 8, 31, 32, 33, 34, 35, 79, 81, 83, 85, 87
Freemasons 23, 83
gender 10, 78, 84
George Bernard Shaw 66
George Luxon 14
George VI Period 49
Girls 22, 30, 31, 33, 34, 67, 84, 85
Glasgow 76, 77
Glyn Road 80, 81, 86
Grange Estate 15
Grange Park Road 11, 107
Gustav Holst 30, 87
Hackney 21, 80, 81
Hammersmith 22, 24, 25, 28, 30, 79, 80, 81, 85, 87

Homerton 21
Hugh Trevor 17, 19, 82
Huguenot 107
Imperial Institute Silk Advisory
    Committee 50
India 23, 24, 33, 80, 83
Italy 43, 46, 51, 52
James I 107
James Patten 12
Japan 46, 52, 56
Jill Adams 67
Joan Ryder 73
John Martin 49
Kensington 24, 35, 37, 38, 82, 84
Kent 7, 11, 52, 57, 64, 88, 112
Kentish Town 12
Lady Dorothy Nevill 28
Lady Emily Hart Dyke 36, 71, 72
Laura Henderson 74, 75
Lea Bridge Station 20
Lea Hall Road 15
Leatherhead 39, 42, 43, 45, 87
Leyton 7, 10, 11, 12, 13, 15, 16, 18, 19, 20,
    21, 22, 26, 29, 79, 81, 83, 86, 88, 89,
    107, 112
Leytonstone 108
Lina Mary 71, 72
Lina Mary Crivellari 71
Lullingstone 7, 35, 43, 45, 46, 47, 51, 52,
    54, 57, 61, 66, 67, 70, 73, 76, 77, 87,
    91, 103
Lullingstone Angora Farm 57
Lulu Guinness 64
Luxon 7, 11, 14, 15, 17, 21, 25, 79, 81
Major R. Field Bibb 63, 67
Manor Road 7, 10, 11, 15, 16, 17, 18, 21,
    28, 29, 107, 108
Margaret Brodie 76, 77
Margaret Lomax 83
Marion Dorn 49
marriage 14, 25, 33, 35, 36, 37, 38, 62, 79,
    81, 83, 84, 85, 112
Martha Mills 112
Mary Benedetta 74
Marylebone 36, 37, 72
Mary Patten 12, 13, 24, 80
Mary Porter 12, 111, 112

Melbourne 82, 86
Millicent Zoë Bond 7
Ministry of Agriculture 60
Miranda Hart 41
moths 28, 42
Mr C. W. Davies 37
Mr Goodale 50, 51
Mrs Crivellari 56, 71, 72
mulberry tree 7, 12, 26, 28, 29, 30, 33, 75,
    77, 87, 108
Myra K. Bishop 35
Norfolk 11, 12, 13, 14, 21, 23, 80, 83, 85,
    112
North Kent Rabbit Breeders Ltd 57
Oliver Augustus 34, 35, 36, 37, 39, 42, 43,
    45, 49, 62, 82, 90, 103
Oliver Guy Hart Dyke 39, 45, 103, 116
Oxford Biography 49
Paulina 30, 67
Poole 21, 22, 23, 24, 28, 87
Port Said 83, 84
Public Health Act 20
Pulham St Mary the Virgin 23, 112
Punjab 23, 24, 82
Queen Mary 47, 49, 77
Rebecca Ann 11, 12, 24, 111, 112
Representation of the People Act 25, 85
Rev. Cyril B. Marshall 37
Rev. John Mills 13, 20, 111, 112
Robert Goodden 69
Rosa Luxemburg 28
Rosemary June Hart Dyke 41
Royal College of Physicians 112
Royal College of Surgeons 112
Royal Horticultural Society 29
Royal Society of Arts 47, 49
RSA 50, 51, 90
Samuel Ryder 73
Sarah Alexander Hart Dyke 41
Saumur 31, 32, 33, 35, 87
Science Museum 47
Second World War 87
sericulture 26, 46, 49, 50, 71, 87
Silk and Rayon Users Association 59
silk farm 7, 49, 51, 52, 53, 57, 67, 70, 71,
    72, 91

silkworms 7, 26, 28, 30, 32, 34, 42, 43, 45,
    46, 51, 54, 55, 77, 87
Sir David Hart Dyke 103
Sir Derek William Hart Dyke 39
Sir Oliver 42, 51, 55, 56, 122
Sir William Hart Dyke 35, 36, 37, 45
social mobility 10, 88
St Paul's Girls' School 22, 30, 33, 34, 84,
    85
Stratford 108, 122
Surrey 29, 39, 85
Sussex 45, 81, 86, 113
Sylvia Christine 17, 21, 38, 79, 84, 85
The Grange 107
Tom Hart Dyke 40, 43, 52, 53, 55, 60, 91
Treyarnon 15, 107, 114
Turkey 43
Vicarage Road 11
Victorian 10, 72
Virginia Woolf 28, 115
Walter Tremayne 17, 25, 33, 38, 79, 83, 84
Walthamstow 17, 18, 19
Warners 50, 51
wedding 8, 35, 36, 37, 38, 39, 43, 52, 69
west London 8, 22, 25, 30, 34, 37
woman 8, 24, 34, 53, 71, 74, 77, 78, 87, 88
women 25, 26, 28, 32, 34, 67, 76, 77, 84,
    85, 87, 88, 90
Women of Empire Pavilion 76
yarn 7, 52, 54, 56, 57
Zoë 7, 8, 9, 10, 11, 13, 17, 19, 21, 22, 23,
    24, 25, 26, 28, 30, 31, 32, 33, 34, 35,
    36, 37, 38, 39, 40, 41, 42, 43, 45, 46,
    47, 49, 50, 51, 52, 53, 54, 55, 56, 57,
    60, 61, 62, 64, 65, 66, 67, 71, 72, 73,
    74, 76, 77, 78, 79, 80, 81, 82, 83, 84,
    85, 86, 87, 88, 89, 90, 91, 103, 107

Unravelling the Yarn

Acknowledgements

Special thanks to:

- The Hart Dyke family for documents and insights.
- Derek Cook for proof-reading draft versions.
- Waltham Forest Archives at Vestry House Museum, Vestry Road, London E17 for access to Leyton records.
- Mill Green Museum, Hatfield, for access to documents of the silk farm at Ayot St Lawrence.
- David Boote, Chair of the Leyton & Leytonstone Historical Society, for his encouragement and guidance.
- Daniella Gorotyák of Grafikai Műhely Illúzió and Attila Halmos of Apolló Média Kft, Baja Hungary for speedy production of proof copies.
- Howard Bailes, Archivist of St Paul's Girls' School, Hammersmith, for curating material from *Paulina*.
- M. Denécheau, Saumur, France, for permission to reproduce photographs of Le Collège des Jeunes Filles.
- David Rose for permission to reproduce the photograph of Mrs Henderson.
- Tom Ryder-Smith for permission to reproduce the photograph of Joan Ryder.
- Glasgow School of Art for assistance with sourcing the image of the Glasgow *Fashion Theatre Women of Empire Pavilion*.
- Flora Smith of Topfoto Ltd for sourcing John Topham's photographs of the Hart Dyke family.
- Lindsay Topping for specially creating Lullingstone Castle and Gate House Lullingstone water-colour sketches.
- Sophie Yeomans for specially taking the photograph of Alburgh church.
- Michael Beck of Karl Dietz Verlag Berlin GMBH for permission to reproduce the image of Rosa Luxemburg's mulberry sprig.
- Lorna Seymour for final proof-reading.
- Lucy Harrison for layout and print management.
- Members of my family and my friends who tolerated, helped or encouraged my preoccupation with this tale!

Unravelling the Yarn